SELECTIONS

FROM

DR. LOW'S WORKS

(1950-1953)

Published by

RECOVERY INTERNATIONAL

Oak Brook, Illinois 60523

ABRAHAM A. LOW

Founder of Recovery, Inc.

This book is dedicated with the deep appreciation and affection of all Recovery members to the memory of the late Dr. Abraham A. Low.

FOREWORD

The articles and comments in this book were written by Dr. Abraham A. Low for the Recovery News which was published every two months by Recovery, Inc. during the years 1950-1953.

Due to the fact that many requests for these articles have been received by Recovery, Inc. they are now being presented in a more permanent binding.

Recovery, Inc. came into existence as a result of many years of research and study by the late Dr. Abraham A. Low. Dr. Low was in an unusually good position to conduct such studies, since from 1931 to 1940 he was the Associate Director and in 1940 and 1941 the Acting Director of the Psychiatric Institute of the University of Illinois.

During these same years he was assistant alienist for the State of Illinois and Associate Professor of Psychiatry at the University of Illinois Medical School. In these various capacities, he saw and treated thousands of nervous and mental patients. As a result of his experience, he founded Recovery in 1937 for the purpose of preventing relapses in former mental patients and chronicity in nervous patients.

Since the decease of Dr. Low in 1954 Recovery International has been operated, managed, supported and controlled by patients and former patients trained in the Recovery Method.

CONTENTS

NATURAL AND ARTIFICIAL MODES OF ACTION
February 1950   1

NERVOUS PATIENTS AND NERVOUS PERSONS
March 1950   6

THE MANIA FOR EXAGGERATION AND PASSION FOR
PREVENTION, May 1950   11

FEELINGS AND BELIEFS, DUALITY AND UNITY
June 1950   16

BLINDSPOTTING AND SPOTLIGHTING, August 1950   22

TOTAL PERSONALITY AND TOTAL SITUATION
September 1950   27

EXPECTATIONS AND DISAPPOINTMENTS
November 1950   33

SELF-SPOTTING AND FOREIGN SPOTTING
December 1950   39

QUOTATIONS FROM DR. LOW'S ADDRESSES
February 1951   44

    1. Identifying Versus Interpretive Diagnoses

    2. Muscular and Mental Habits

    3. Self-Endorsement and Predisposition

    4. Bodily Tools and Mental Attitudes

EXCERPTS FROM DR. LOW'S ADDRESSES, March 1951   49

    1. Self-Importance and Group-Importance

    2. The "Misunderstood" and "Unappreciated" Patient

EXCERPTS FROM DR. LOW'S ADDRESSES, May 1951   53

    1. "The Patient's Confusions"—Chance or Purpose?

    2. "It Is Real; I Don't Imagine It."

EXCERPTS FROM DR. LOW'S ADDRESSES, June 1951   58

    The Patient's Disabilities, Will or Fate?

TO SPOT IS TO KNOW THAT YOU DON'T KNOW
September 1951 62

THE PHILOSOPHY OF RECOVERY, INC., November 1951 67
Order, Beliefs, Convictions

THE PRACTICE OF "STEPPING IN AND TAKING OVER"
December 1951 73

This volume, selections from Dr. Low's works, 1950-1953, is a combination of the two red books, Volume I and Volume II, and it includes all the articles that were contained in them. The articles that were contained in Volume II begin on page 78.

SOME FACTS THE DENTIST OUGHT TO KNOW ABOUT
HIMSELF, February 1952 78

QUOTATIONS FROM DR. LOW'S ADDRESSES, March 1952 ... 86
1. Tenseness and Self-Consciousness
2. The Shame of Sabotage
3. The Patient Is An Apprentice, Not a Master

DR. LOW'S COLUMN, May 1952 92
1. Possibilities and Probabilities. How to Spot Them
2. The Dual and Divided Will

I AM TIRED ALL THE TIME, September 1952 97

THE WILL TO FEAR, December 1952 100

DR. LOW'S COMMENTS ON
EXAMPLES OF RECOVERY PRACTICE

EXAMPLES OF RECOVERY PRACTICE, June 1952 105
1. Denver, Colorado—Sherley M.
2. Chicago, Illinois—Frank R.
3. Evansville, Indiana—Florence L.
4. Brighton, Michigan—Mary Alice L.

EXAMPLES OF RECOVERY PRACTICE, August 1952 111

1. Denver, Colorado—Kate S.

2. Muscatine, Iowa—Charles F.

3. Muscatine, Iowa—Vivian N.

4. Brighton, Michigan—Mary Alice L.

5. Brighton, Michigan—Peggy N.

EXAMPLES OF RECOVERY PRACTICE, September 1952 117

1. Chicago, Illinois—Phil C.

2. Chicago, Illinois—Ann L.

3. Muscatine, Iowa—Ernest H.

4. Brighton, Michigan—Marge H.

5. Brighton, Michigan—Ruth H.

6. Brighton, Michigan—Treasure R.

EXAMPLES OF RECOVERY PRACTICE, November 1952 125

1. Chicago, Illinois—Frank R.

2. Brighton, Michigan—Jerry L.

EXAMPLES OF RECOVERY PRACTICE, May 1953 130

1. Brighton, Michigan—Treasure R.

DR. LOW'S COLUMN
NATURAL AND ARTIFICIAL MODES OF ACTION

Winnifred, on the Saturday afternoon panel, recalled a significant recent experience. "Lunching and daydreaming, I noticed something small and dark on a piece of lettuce. Dreaming as I did I paid little attention and took another forkful of salad and a bite of bread before I fully realized that it was a worm. I whisked it from the plate and jumped up to protest to the waitress. Then I spotted my reaction and felt I had permitted myself to get upset over a harmless little worm and knew that if I hadn't known I wouldn't have been any the worse off for it. Then I took the worm off the plate and was ready to continue the meal when it struck me that where there is one worm there may be more. I stopped eating. By this time my stomach felt queasy and trembly. But it seemed to me that to give up eating altogether would not be good Recovery practice so I finished my bread and drank some milk. I even took a few more bits of the salad. And yet, my stomach has always been squeamish. All a person has to do is to speak of an accident or a sick stomach or snakes and I am ill. Before my Recovery training, I would have rushed to the bathroom, would have thrown up the food and would have gargled several times and would have felt nauseated all day. Also it would have been a long time before I could bring myself to eat lettuce, spinach, or any leafy vegetable for fear it might hide a bug..."

Winnifred found a worm in her food and was ready to jump at the waitress but controlled her temper. She then interrupted the meal but resumed it soon because she thought, "to give up eating altogether would not be good Recovery practice." I shall readily admit that "Recovery practice" disapproves the "common practice" to raise a fuss and jump at people, and when Winnifred refrained from making a scene she gave an inspiring example of temper control which was an authentic piece of "Recovery practice." But when she reflected that the same practice required a person to indulge in the heroics and acrobatics of forcing contaminated food down the throat she obviously misinterpreted our principles of self-discipline. In trying to perform an heroic act, she violated the basic Recovery rule to be average, that means, to avoid being heroic, saintly or angelic. Practicing exceptional behavior of this kind is the very reverse of "good Recovery practice.'' Recovery stands for averageness and shuns extremism. Winnifred, desirous of establishing an excellent record of perfect Recovery behavior, defaulted on the supreme principle of Recovery's philosophy which frowns on excellence, perfectionism and extremism in the daily round of average existence.

When Winnifred caught sight of the worm on her plate the situation was one of an affront, an insult, a frustration.

Situations of this kind are *not routine but challenging*. They challenge you to make a decision and to take a position. There were three possible ways of meeting the challenge: Winnifred could have ''jumped at'' the waitress, could have released a burst of violent protests, perhaps threatening to report the incident to the health department and to sue for damages. Had she done that her position would have been that of the angry, aggressive temper. The second possibility was that she might have become so frightened and disgusted by the experience that, in utter dismay and revulsion of feelings, she would have left the table, paid the bill and rushed out of the restaurant. This would have been the position of the fearful, retreating temper. The third position she could have taken was to call the waitress asking her to replace the dish. This would have been a realistic, non-temperamental approach. Had Winnifred chosen any of these three positions she would have done what the average person might be expected to do under similar circumstances. Her position, whether temperamental or realistic, would still have been average. When, however, she decided to ignore the worm and to continue the meal she took an heroic position, stepped out of the domain of averageness and chose the exceptional approach.

It will be helpful to you to know that every significant situation in your life may challenge you to choose between the three positions I mentioned. When you are irritated by your mother or your boss, by your government or by a traffic jam, by a fly settling on your cheek or a noisy neighbor disturbing your peace, in all these situations you are free to choose between the two *extreme positions* of the angry or fearful temper and the *middle position* of realistic control. This arrangement of situations into three discreet portions is characteristic of everything that grows and lives. What is called the ''order of things'' or ''ordered existence'' merely means that life is so arranged that things and acts run from one extreme to the other, passing through a middle ground in which

2

the items lose their extreme size, duration or intensity and reach moderate or modest proportions. That part of your life, for instance, which is called appetite runs from immoderate to minimal desire for food with a region of modest craving in the middle. Similarly, the trees of a forest are ordered or distributed in such a series that the tall and small specimens meet in a middle ground of moderate-sized trees. All feelings, sensations, beliefs, impulses run this common gamut from extreme intensity through moderate excitement to minimal responses. The same principle of distribution holds good for symptoms, temper, intelligence, memory and attention, talents and skills, character and disposition. They all run from one extreme to the other passing through a middle ground of modest, moderate and common manifestations. This type of arrangement of things and actions into a broad middle ground flanked by two narrow extremes, being the commonly found order of nature, has been called the *"natural" or "normal" mode of distribution.* If a forest should consist of tall trees only the distribution would be termed "unnatural" or "abnormal." This mode of distribution could not be produced by nature; it would require the art of the gardener and would be artistic or artificial. Nature knows no uniformity; it lives and grows by variety. Its principle is that of the natural or normal distribution. The opposite of nature is manufacture or technique. Technique can produce thousands of cars in one lot all of them looking exactly alike. This is the technical, unnatural, artificial mode of distribution. An existence, "ordered" largely by technique, is bound to drift into an artificial mode of living.

Winnifred's determination to ignore the worm on her plate was either heroic or angelic or saintly. But it was not natural. The determination, although containing the elements of Will (to exercise supreme control) and feeling (of nausea), was in the main guided by a thought. It was the realization that here was a unique chance to practice Recovery principles to the limit of possibility. The thought had the character of a rare inspiration, of an extraordinary opportunity, perhaps of singular brilliance. It was romanto-intellectual, exceptional and extreme, not natural and average. Ordinarily, the mental productions of the average individual have their natural distribution. At times, they are brilliant flashes; at other times, they are outright stupidities. But the majority of his intellectual exertions are just average, lacking the "divine spark," moving along lazily in the tracks of a broad middle ground of sound but colorless realistic reasoning, revealing neither intellectual brilliance nor mental sluggishness. The same type of natural distribution governs the average person's record of self-control. His self-discipline may sometimes reach the height of supreme determination, or it may occasionally sink to the depth of extreme vacillation, but the majority of his acts sprawl along a middle course of average limited control. A person who is *always* self-possessed and reserved, or *always* shrinking and cringing, has lost the natural distribution of his traits; he has eliminated everything from his action that spells natural movement, average variety and healthy change. He may have acquired the grandeur of a "lone eagle," or the distinction of a self-sufficient hermit, or the glory of an invincible hero, but he is not a warm, natural and human person. His expressions and actions are rigid, mechanical, one-sided and extreme performances. His traits have an unnatural and artificial distribution.

You who know Winnifred will agree that she is undoubtedly warm, human and natural. There is very little artificiality in her make-up. But she is a nervous patient, and nervous patients tend to be extremists with regard to their symptoms when they are still sick and with regard to the practice of rules after they have improved. As long as they still suffer the tortures of sensations and obsessions they have the extremist fear that they are doomed *forever.* When, after improving, they experience the delight of comfort and relaxation they are likewise extreme in their certainty that they will *never* be sick again. There is little or no middle ground of moderate caution or moderate doubt. It is either black despair all the time, or heavenly bliss without interruption. Their actions, thoughts and impulses know one manner of movement only: the abrupt jump from one extreme to the other, from torturing tenseness to complete relaxation, from the threat of doom to the promise of happiness. The leisurely walk through the middle ground of average experience is unknown to them. Their aches and pressures and fatigues are invariably "unendurable" and "intolerable." The dizziness is never a plain and average reaction but always "the worse ever." The symptoms *never* stop and are *always* of maximum intensity. As the years and months pass the practice of thinking in terms of extreme experiences becomes a deep rooted habit. The entire area of thought is then steeped in the philosophy of extremism. In Recovery they learn to conquer their symptoms. They regain their self-confidence and retrieve their capacity for relaxation and enjoyment. But the habit of thinking in terms of extremism may persist. Control, then, becomes super-control; spotting turns into an heroic effort to track down every tiny vestige of sabotage. To their minds, health must be complete relaxation, absolute freedom from symptoms, utter absence of discomfort. By the same token, practice of rules means practicing them all the time, in all places, on all occasions, relentlessly, without compromise, without qualification. Winnifred answered this general description of the nervous patient. When she was ill she viewed her symptoms with extreme pessimism; when she recovered her health she thought of control in terms of extreme self-discipline. What she will have to learn is the art of moving in a middle ground of average, natural and human thought and action, steering clear of the unnatural extremes of wanting *always* to be perfection and *never* to tolerate deficiency.

DR. LOW'S COLUMN
NERVOUS PATIENTS AND NERVOUS PERSONS

Gertrude was elected representative to the Good Will Club of the organization for which she works. As such she had to attend meetings in which she was the only woman member. This alone made her very uncomfortable, and when she was to take the floor she "became tense and had all sorts of symptoms, palpitations, tremors, air-hunger and the thought that I simply can't do this. But with my Recovery training I knew that this was merely discomfort and I can bear it and make my muscles do the job of addressing the crowd. But one day the Club decided to hold a raffle for the benefit of an employee who was chronically ill. Somebody had to run the raffle and, lo and behold, they picked me to organize it. I got scared and thought that I certainly can't do that. But I spotted this immediately as the fear of making mistakes and knew that I had to have the courage to make mistakes. I accepted and felt proud that I had the nerve to tackle this business. And here I was a nervous patient, and many of those present refused to take on that responsibility, and as far as I know they were not nervous patients..."

Gertrude was assigned a difficult and responsible task. She accepted and felt proud of the confidence she inspired and the distinction she gained but wondered why the others who "were not nervous patients" had refused while she who "was a nervous patient" had accepted. When she spoke of her reaction she mentioned that when she was asked to attend meetings as a representative she had "all sorts of symptoms...and the thought that I simply can't do this." Later, when she was chosen for the job of organizing the raffle she again "got scared and thought that I certainly can't do that." These statements so well expressed by Gertrude point up the chief difficulty of the "nervous patient" whose main characteristic is to be scared of responsibilities which means to lack the confidence and courage to assume a task. The fact remains, however, that the others who "were not nervous patients" were by no means oozing courage and confidence, and the prospect of being offered a responsible assignment did not seem to rouse their enthusiasm or fire their ambition. From this and many kindred observations which I am currently able to make I conclude that the person who is not a nervous patient differs little from that specimen of humanity who happens to be afflicted with a nervous ailment. The one is a *"nervous person"*; the other is a *"nervous patient."* In the instance quoted by Gertrude, the nervous persons shied away from responsibilities, the nervous patient faced and braved them.

I do not know the men and women who work for the company which employs Gertrude. Nevertheless, assuming they are an average group, I will not hesitate to assert that all of them are nervous persons. This means that all of them are, in varying degrees, tense, self-conscious, unsure of themselves. I can make this statement with confidence because the many people which I meet or know, including myself, give ample evidence of inner restlessness, lack of assurance, preoccupation and lowered spontaneity. And these qualities connote nervousness; and people possessing them are nervous persons which means that all average men and women who do not happen to be heroes, saints or angels belong in this category of nervous persons. The clearest evidence of this universal nervousness I obtain when I observe myself. I then notice that it would be easy for me to duplicate most of the symptoms, dispositions and attitudes of which my patients complain. There is a difference, of course, between my reactions and those of my patients. They develop severe vicious cycles, and I produce none or very mild ones; they go into panics and tantrums while I avoid or escape them; they release volleys of complaints, and I practice silence. Other differences come to mind: The symptoms of my patients have gained intensity, and mine are calm experiences; theirs are protracted agonies, and mine are merely transient annoyances. If you list all these differences which obtain between me and my patients you may be inclined to infer that what distinguishes a nervous person, like I, from a nervous patient, like Gertrude, is the capacity to release tantrums and panics and vicious cycles and to endow symptoms with a high degree of intensity, with long duration and endless verbal explosions. That this is not true is obvious because you and I know many relatives, friends and neighbors who display, occasionally or frequently, all the features which I mentioned, from intense panics to never-ending complaint-marathons, and yet are merely nervous persons instead of nervous patients. What, then, is the basic difference between the two groups?

An intelligent answer to this question cannot be given unless you know what the word "basic" means. If you watch the behavior of a large body of water, let me say, Lake Michigan, you will find that the surface is frequently smooth, calm, serene. If that is the case we say the lake is at peace. At times, however, you will observe that the lake develops motion, at first gentle ripples, than rolling waves, finally spouting billows. The water is now active, perhaps slightly agitated but not turbulent. On some days a storm rises. The waves become tempestuous, raging for hours or days, and the body of water appears shaken with wild passion and fierce commotion. This is what you might call a violent symptom or uncontrolled tantrum, intense, protracted, raving. Should you be asked to describe the general nature and character of the lake you might explain that, basically and fundamentally, it is a fine piece of water with excellent opportunities for recreation, a valuable reservoir for sea-food, a convenient traffic lane for navigation, and above all, an unparalleled asset in point of scenic beauty. These, you will add, are the basic features of the lake. But some phases of its nature and action, you will continue, admit of a less glowing description: there are gales and squalls and mighty storms lashing the shores, and ships go aground and human lives are destroyed, etc. etc.... In giving an account of this sort you made a pointed distinction between the basic nature of the lake and certain of its phases which, being *phasic,* are not *basic* to its fundamental character. Essentially, you took the position that in giving the description of an object you meant to stress what is at its base and foundation, not what are merely certain phases of its behavior. Basically, you wanted to point out, Lake Michigan is a marvel of beauty and bounty, but phasically it may at times be forbidding and treacherous.

When Gertrude arrived at the self-depreciating conclusion that being a nervous patient she was less qualified for a responsible job than her co-workers who "were not nervous patients" she overemphasized certain phases of her behavior, ignoring or minimizing what was at its base. Her judgment was focused on the shifting and phasic elements of her conduct, not on its permanent and basic foundation. On the other hand, her co-workers, when passing judgment on their own qualities, were inclined to play down their phasic defects and to play up their basic merits. They did not deny their disturbances and defects. They knew and did not blink the fact that they had occasional palpitations and air-hunger. But that did not suggest to them the wild idea that their circulation and respiration were basically damaged. Instead, they were certain that the present disturbance was merely an occasional or momentary phase of their basically sound behavior. At times it happened that some of them went into the living room to fetch an object and stood there not remembering what they had come for. Or, there was the experience that after parking the automobile they forgot where they had left it. On such occasions it was perfectly clear to them that the present act of forgetting was merely a transient phase of their memory function and that the latter was basically intact and dependable. This was different in the case of Gertrude. Whenever incidents of this character occurred in her life she was likely to condemn her functions as basically and fundamentally untrustworthy, disintegrating, defective. You see the difference: Gertrude had about the same type of experiences as her co-workers, defects of memory, disturbances of organ functions, scares, tempers, undesirable impulses and what not. But whereas Gertrude indicted her basic functions her co-workers put the blame on some phase of their conduct only. Basically, they approved of their behavior. If they condemned at all, their condemnations were directed at some of its phasic portions only.

The incident which Gertrude reported on the panel was of recent occurrence. At the time it happened she had lost her fears and her disturbing sensations and had made such a good adjustment that the co-workers thought her capable of being entrusted with a responsible task. Which means that they had trust in her capacities. Had they known her previous ailment they might have marvelled at the thoroughness of her recovery. They had faith in her basic qualities but Gertrude had none. She knew that she still had difficulties. She knew that occasionally her palpitations, sweats and weaknesses returned. True, she had to admit that they were no longer intense, no longer sustained or incapacitating. In other words, she had graduated from the status of a nervous patient to that of a nervous person. This was the manner in which those of her co-workers judged her who knew or might have known of her nervous ailment. It is also the manner in which I judge her. But Gertrude thought otherwise. To her, the recurring symptoms were a reminder that she had once gone through torturing agonies. Now she was seized with the fear that the agonies might return and stay with her. The recurring nervous symptoms made her anticipate a return of the nervous ailment. This is what we call the stigma of nervous illness—once nervously ill, always nervously ill. To feel stigmatized means to experience a basic self-distrust. Gertrude distrusted her Self because it still produced nervous symptoms. But nervous symptoms do not signify that the one having them is a nervous patient. Nor do they mean the threatening return of a nervous ailment. They merely indicate that average people, being neither heroes, saints or angels, are nervous persons. All of them have nervous reactions; all of them are, in varying degrees, tense, self-conscious, unsure of themselves. And their tenseness, self-consciousness and lack of assurance may at any time give rise to any kind of nervous symptoms. Gertrude had recovered, that is, she had again become an average nervous person. But not knowing that average persons have nervous symptoms she feared a return of her ailment when her symptoms "kicked up" again. What she and all my patients will have to learn is that nervousness and nervous symptoms are universal and average and that to get well means to become again an average nervous person who experiences nervous reactions in many phases of his life but has implicit confidence in the trustworthiness of his basic functions.

DR. LOW'S COLUMN
THE MANIA FOR EXAGGERATION AND PASSION FOR PREVENTION

Ada, on the Saturday panel, related that one day last summer she felt a mild pain in the right foot. "I did not notice any swelling or redness so I paid no further attention to it. The pain grew worse but I still didn't see anything so I thought it was nerves. Toward evening the pain got so strong that I had to take off my shoes and wear slippers. By this time I felt quite uncomfortable but I still felt it was a nervous pain and even joked about it to my family. The pain got worse again at night and I could hardly sleep. The following morning when I looked at the foot it was red and swollen, but somehow I still thought it was nerves. Next day the pain was almost unbearable and I decided to call the family physician. He called it an infection and prescribed bedrest and soaking in hot water. All of this time I suffered but was calm. But then the neighbors heard about my foot trouble, and they came to visit me. One said I know you suffer from a nervous condition but, honest, this looks as if all the nerves in your foot had burst. Another visitor said, how can your doctor expect that simple hot water will ever cure a foot like this? A relative said, why, with a foot like that you should have penicillin. I became fearful now and thought I would have to go to the hospital and I would have blood poisoning and the foot will have to be amputated. Finally I called the doctor again, and when he examined the foot he reassured me, and in a few days I was on my feet again. Before I had my Recovery training I would have listened to the women and would have worked myself up to a hysteria...."

Ada felt a pain in the right foot and "thought it was nerves." The pain got worse, and a swelling and redness appeared but she "still thought it was nerves." Finally, when the distress grew in intensity, she called the doctor who considered it a mild infection and prescribed simple remedies. Up to this point the situation was dealt with quietly and dispassionately both by Ada and the doctor. Both made calm observations and gave sober opinions. This changed, however, when neighbors and relatives appeared on the scene. They were loud and dramatic and alarmist and communicated their hysteria to Ada who now conceived dreadful visions of blood poisoning, hospitalization and amputation of the leg. Even so, Ada managed to shake off the hysteria promptly and recovering her sober mode of thinking summoned the physician again and was cured in the space of a few days.

I know Ada's physician whose professional competence is unquestioned. And if he thought of a mild infection which required nothing more complicated than hot dressings; moreover, if on a second visit he saw no reason to change his diagnosis I shall not hesitate to assume that the swelling and redness were of a moderate degree. The fact that Ada was on her feet within a few days supports my view of an innocent disturbance. Why, then, did the neighbors and relatives think of an emergency that spelled nothing less than mortal danger? Why this senseless passion for seeing danger in things harmless?

I also happen to know some of Ada's neighbors and relatives whom I consider ordinary folk, good natured and well intentioned, ready to help and give comfort. As such they belong in the class of average people. The question may be asked: Are ordinary, average people in the habit of magnifying harmless events into gruesome dangers? Are average people inclined to be irresponsible alarmists? Unfortunately, the answer is an unqualifed YES.

What we call average people are persons who, though generally realistic, have nevertheless a strong tendency to indulge in those types of sentimentalisms and emotionalisms which I call romanto-intellectualist. In the instance of Ada's foot ailment, these worthy people displayed a rank romanticism when they saw in a simple condition of swelling and redness the evidence of something extraordinary and exciting and extremely dangerous. They exhibited a lush intellectualism when they recklessly suggested that they knew the proper remedy and the physician did not, that they were right and he was wrong. The romanticist rejoices in the sight of excitements, stormy events and dangerous situations; the intellectualist relishes a self-imposed mission to prevent storms and dangers. The one has a mania for preposterous exaggeration, the other has a passion for ludicrous prevention. Ada's visitors were what most undisciplined people tend to be: past masters of the gentle art of exaggeration and champions of the tricky game of prevention. In other words, they were consummate romanto-intellectualists.

Life is essentially a matter of routine performance. The heart and lungs perform the routine of circulation and respiration, the stomach and intestines that of digestion, the nervous system that of receiving impressions and releasing impulses. If the routine goes on undisturbed we speak of physical, mental and social health. The healthy *routine* may at any time be interrupted by mild *complications* or severe *emergencies*. Complications can be corrected either by the passage of time or by simple remedial measures. For instance, a person having palpitations may either wait till they will disappear (time taking care of the complication) or put an ice cap to the chest (simple remedy). If the complication is of a social nature, for instance, friction developing among employees, the employer may, similarly, either decide to let time heal the breach, or call in the contending parties and remedy the situation by a simple ruling. In either case, routine complications were treated by means of routine measures. This is impossible if an emergency is on. If a man collapses or a fire rages it would be silly or criminal to trust to time or to simple measures to prevent the collapse or to stem the conflagration. Emergencies demand instant, perhaps heroic intervention. What is called judgment is mainly the art of distinguishing clearly between simple complications and severe emergencies. A person lacking this discriminating judgment is bound to muddle or even ruin his life through the folly of treating emergencies with routine measures or simple complications with emergency procedures. When Ada decided to let time take care of her sore foot she exhibited sound judgment and good discrimination. When her neighbors and relatives suggested emergency measures their judgment was poor and their discrimination nil. She, the nervous patient, was well adjusted; they, the nervous persons, were grotesquely deficient in adjustment. She was calm, they were hysterical. They were by no means hysterical patients but, emphatically, they were hysterical persons. It is an annoying and dangerous habit of hysterical persons to mistake complications for emergencies and to resort to heroic and dramatic measures when nothing more than simple remedies are called for.

Hysterical persons are average people with an unbridled bent for romanto-intellectualist thought, action and expression. Driven by an unquenched thirst for thrills and excitements, they see emergencies in every paltry occurrence. Magnifying innocent events into physical or social emergencies of vast proportions they are always on the jump to prevent a threat. In the course of time they acquire a *mania for exaggeration* and a *passion for prevention*. The women who immediately "knew" that Ada's swelling was a threat to her life and urged prompt prevention were hysterical persons though average people.

Prior to going through the discipline of Recovery training my patients are hysterical persons. As such, they have embraced the philosophy of reckless exaggeration and the policy of fortuitous prevention. Magnifying their complaints is the very breath of their life. They feel tired and speak of "utter exhaustion." Going through a period of disturbed sleep they insist they "haven't slept a wink for weeks or months." They notice a few streaks of blood in their stools and exclaim dramatically that "the blood just gushes out of me." They describe a perspiration of ordinary dimensions and add that "the sweat comes out every single pore of mine." They have "millions of the most terrible sensations," their fingers "feel just like icicles," and they do not hesitate to state with solemn emphasis that "if I survived yesterday, honestly, I must be made of iron." In one of their many surgical operations the appendix "was just caught in time before it burst," and in another "all the intestines were already swimming in pus when the surgeon went in." Theirs is the "only case of this kind," and "the pain is more than anybody could possibly stand," and "nobody can make me believe that I can be cured after so many years of suffering." But if their agonies are so overwhelming and their disturbances of such a gigantic nature, instant intervention is, of course, imperative, and so my patients, prior to their Recovery training, are all and sundry hysterical persons, addicted to the mania for exaggeration and the passion for prevention.

I still remember the time when hysterical behavior was generally considered to occur among the uncultured and illiterate only or mainly. The intelligent classes were supposed to be immune to the coarse notions of mass superstition and proof against the crude antics of mob thinking. Today this has changed. All you have to do is listen to the radio or to read your daily newspaper and you will be treated to a hodgepodge of absurd exaggerations coming from professionals, not from fishwives, who will tell you that this great country of ours has 15 million of children with marked defects of hearing, an equal number with significant disturbances of sight, 8 million other children who are seriously crippled, close to 10 million adults who are afflicted with incapacitating arthritis. They tell you that two of every three persons die of heart disease, that about half the adult population are the victims of mental ailments, chronic alcoholism, delinquency or similar evidence of abnormal behavior. Let me assure you that nobody is in a position to have even remotely accurate information on the incidence of these ailments and defects. And if you read such fantastically inflated horror statistics be certain they are either wild guesses or feverish fabrications doled out by men who are convulsed with the mania for exaggeration. Unfortunately, these promoters of doom yarns are also a prey to the passion for prevention. They flood street cars and buses and subways with flamboyant posters reminding you that "every three minutes a person dies of cancer" which may be a fact but is an extremely vicious and devilishly cruel suggestion, particularly if followed by the malicious warning that "You may be next." Other members of the tribe solicit your support for a crusade against a certain painful affliction exhorting you to "give before it hurts." I could go on indefinitely describing the pernicious nature of this modern version of the mania for exaggeration and passion for prevention were it not that the mere mention of these horror statistics is apt to cause a revulsion of feeling. If I dwelt on this statistical trickery at all it was done because many of my patients, after hearing the tales of horror over the radio or reading them in print, developed severe reactions until I prevailed on them to ignore all alarmist pronouncements of professional promoters regardless of how worthy the cause may be in whose hire the prophets of disaster plied their sordid trade. Ada demonstrated how irresponsible chit-chat of this kind ought to be treated. She listened politely to the doom message of her visitors but went resolutely her own way which is the way of Recovery, an organization which is dead set against all alarmism be it based on the phony statistics of professional hucksters or on the honest chatter of gossipy housewives. In Recovery she was trained to spot and stop hysterical behavior and to steer clear of the mania for exaggeration and the passion for prevention.

DR. LOW'S COLUMN
FEELINGS AND BELIEF, DUALITY AND UNITY

Margaret, on the Saturday panel, recalled an occasion in which a customer asked for skirt shields to keep skirts from wrinkling. "I did not know what these shields were and where they were kept. So I asked the girl in charge of stock if she could tell me where they were. She said, 'Do you really mean to say you don't know yet where these things are kept?' Then she showed me the drawer which was for the shields, and I realized I should have known because I had sold some of them recently. That made me feel embarrassed because I had made a fool of myself, and I also felt provoked and thought who does she think she is talking to me like that? I was ready to come back with a sharp remark but then I spotted this as temper and said to myself, I am not going to work myself up, and if she thinks she is smart and I am dumb, well, I have learned in Recovery to be average and not to mind making mistakes. Then I went on helping my customer and thought nothing more of my feelings. . . . ''

Margaret did not know where to look for a skirt shield, and asked the girl in charge of stock—let us call her Lillian—to show her where to find it. Lillian obliged Margaret showing her the drawer which contained the article. This was cooperation and team-work which means group-mindedness. Had nothing else happened we should not hesitate to call Lillian an essentially group-minded person. Unfortunately, something else did happen. In granting Margaret's request, Lillian asked, "Do you *really* mean to say you *don't know yet* where these things are kept?" This inquiry, though couched in tolerably courteous language, contains nevertheless a good deal of discourteous innuendo. By implication, Lillian said: You have been working in this store for several weeks, and it cannot be the *real* truth that you have *not yet* learned where the shields are. A little child, with a mere trace of intelligence and memory, would learn faster. If we read this meaning into Lillian's remark we shall agree that it was heavily spiced with irony and plainly meant to hurt Margaret's feelings. If this is so, we must assume that Lillian had the will to help and the will to hurt at the same time, that she expressed group-mindedness and self-mindedness in the same act, good-will and ill-will in the same breath. Which indicates that Lillian's behavior was governed by two contradictory wills, the one group-oriented, the other starkly individualistic. This accords well with what I have stressed repeatedly, namely, that in this imperfect world of ours, there is no purity of character, personality and will. The average human being who is neither sainty nor heroic nor angelic, is served by two wills, ruled by two characters and obsessed of two personalities. The average person is *dual*, not *unified*.

Lillian could have acted differently. She could have shown the drawer to Margaret, saying, "Here it is. Any time you will be in trouble, just ask me, and I shall be glad to help you if I can." Had she done that, she would have expressed, both in act and phrasing, a unified will, an integrated personality, a consistent character. No doubt, she could have adopted this unified course of conduct. If she did not we must conclude that she *preferred* another course. She preferred or chose a mode of behavior in which she could display, at will, both courtesy and discourtesy, kindliness and churlishness, service and domination. Her preference was for duality, not for unity of action.

If I speak of unity and duality I do not refer to any profound and complex philosophical teaching. What I have in mind is the fact that everybody demands of his fellows—perhaps not so much of himself—that there must be no *double-talking* nor *double-dealing*. The group does not require or expect you to be helpful and generous all the time. You may on occasion refuse to be accommodating or courteous. At times, you may even be rude and aggressive without incurring disapproval, provided you have some acceptable reson for your antagonistic attitude. But you must not permit yourself to be courteous in language and rude in action or vice versa in one and the same performance, no matter what may be your reason. This double-dealing will not be forgiven by the average person who, sensing the duality of conduct—in others—is offended by what he considers duplicity. The offense is experienced as an insult to the intellect and a hurt to one's feelings. Margaret expressed the situation clearly when she said that Lillian's behavior "made me *feel* embarrassed...and I also *felt* provoked." The implication was that her feelings were hurt by Lillian's act of double-dealing. Margaret's subsequent comment that "if she thinks she is smart and I am dumb" indicates that she also felt her intellect was insulted. You may be inclined to pass off Lillian's "talking out of turn" as a triviality and to condemn

Margaret's response as excessive sensitiveness. But the fact remains that, on an average, people resent having their intellect insulted and their feelings hurt by what they please to judge as dual behavior, be it ever so trivial. The average person demands unification and reacts sharply against duality—unfortunately, in others mainly.

I told you repeatedly that your daily life consists chiefly of trivialities. You may be certain that the bulk of your talk, action and feeling are what most of your daily experience is: trivial. But if trivialities are likely to wound your feelings and insult your intellect they may be trivial to others but not to you. To you they become most significant. For nervous patients particularly it is of the utmost significance to shield their sensibilities from being assaulted too frequently or too harshly. Let my patients' feelings be merely scratched or glanced, and the result will be symptoms and suffering. Let their intellect be merely mildly doubted or subtly questioned, and temper tantrums may be released. The trivial encounter between Margaret and Lillian demonstrates that what people consider double-action is most apt to inflict hurt and injury to a sensitive soul. And my patients are without exception sensitive souls. They are highly sensitized to hidden meanings, vague implications and suggestive remarks. They wince in response to innocent pranks, harmless irony and good natured teasing. Consider the meaning of teasing. If you tease a person you may mean and usually do mean no harm. The words which you use may be wholly inoffensive, your tone of voice may indicate warmth and sympathy; the smile on your face may testify to the essentially friendly attitude expressed in the act. Yet, the hidden meaning and indirect implication of the performance are that you do not treat your "victim" with respect, that you do not take him seriously, You are kind and warm and sympathetic in your approach, but at the same time you treat your conversational partner as a baby, refusing or failing to respect his intellect as mature and his feelings as important. The person whom you chose as target for teasing may notice the underlying kindness, but he will not overlook the implied lack of respect for his personal importance. As a teaser you act double, befriending and torturing a person in one and the same utterance. And if the individual whom you tease is a sensitive soul his feelings will be hurt and his intellect insulted by your dual approach. It may still be a triviality but oh, how painful it can be. Lillian merely teased Margaret, or she was merely ironical. Whether it was the one or the other, in essence, it was a trifling affair. But Margaret was provoked by the dual behavior and escaped serious disturbance only because in Recovery she was trained to spot feelings of self-importance as temper and through spotting, to cut short symptoms. Recovery had enabled her to have her feelings exposed to the acid of dual behavior without getting them corroded, without having them even so much as ruffled, except for a brief instant. Having spotted successfully the triviality of the event she dismissed it and was calm.

What precisely was the nature of the feeling which was provoked and insulted and hurt by the ironical thrust which Lillian levelled against Margaret? I have spoken to you about the meaning of feelings repeatedly. And while neither I nor anybody else are able to give an exhaustive statement of what feelings are, nevertheless, a reasonably correct explanation can be attempted. Having thus, with due humility, stated the difficulty of the task let me now tell you, not what feelings are but what my patients ought to know about them. What you should know is that feelings are (1) predominantly physiological which we shall call physical, (2) predominantly psychological which we shall call mental. The *physical feelings* are mainly in the nature of sensations. It is with your senses that you feel the hardness or softness of wood (touch), the brightness or paleness of colors (vision), the pleasing or shrill character of a sound (hearing), the sweet or sour quality of food (taste), the agreeable or disagreeable odor of a substance (smell). These feelings are conveyed to you through the so-called five senses. There are other physical feelings: heat and cold, wetness and dryness, shivers and shudders, pain and pressure, pullings and twisting, dizziness and faintness, and the well nigh inexhaustible host of disturbing sensations with which you have acquired a very painful familiarity. I take it you will understand now what is meant by phyical feelings. If you do, then, you will realize that feelings of this kind can be irritated but not hurt in the sense of being provoked or insulted. Mental feelings are subject to hurts and provocations and insults. I have dealt with these mental feelings in an address which was published under the title of "Temper Masquerading as Feeling" (Recovery News, March 1949). There I told you that the mental feelings can be grouped under three headings: sympathy, apathy, antipathy. I can tell you now that all three are closely linked to *beliefs*. You show sympathy toward somebody who you *believe* is close to you or who you feel (believe) is in distress. The same feelings of sympathy you may direct toward yourself experiencing self-love, self-pity, self-complacency, self-importance, self-respect. That these are beliefs (in one's or someone's worth) requires no comment. Beliefs of a similar nature enter into the composition of the apathetic and antipathic feelings. In apathy you are swayed by the belief that things or persons or yourself are worthless, unimportant, uninspiring, uninteresting. In antipathy, you are repelled by yourself or someone, and the result is that you fear or resent or are disgusted with or revolted by yourself or another person. And fear presupposes the belief in danger; and resentment implies the belief that somebody is wrong or did wrong; and similar beliefs are at the base of disgust or discouragement or other antipathic feelings. I hope I made it clear to you that when you claim that your feelings are hurt, what you actually mean is that some cherished belief of yours has been doubted, questioned, ignored, rejected or, worse yet, ridiculed, treated with irony, not taken seriously. The beliefs which you cherish most are that your opinion is relevant, your judgment mature, your action vital, your conduct worthy. If a person, directly or implicitly, contradicts any of these beliefs he or she indicates that they do not share them, that they consider them incorrect, childish, unbalanced, out of focus, not worth being taken seriously. If this happens, then your (mental) feelings are hurt, which means that one of your cherished or pet beliefs has been offended. That mental feelings are the closest related to beliefs is evident from the manner in which we identify religious beliefs with religious feelings. There is no difference in meaning whether you say, "I believe my prayer was heard" or, "I feel it was heard." Similarly, when we say, "I feel secure (or insecure)", what we actually mean is, "I believe I am secure (or insecure)." The relationship between mental feelings and beliefs is most conspicuous in the case of temper. You feel that somebody did you wrong, and this feeling assuredly is a belief.

You will now be in a better position to understand the trivial but painful scene in which Margaret's "feelings" were hurt by Lillian. Lillian treated Margaret with courtesy in action but with irony in words. Her act expressed a measure of respect, but her ironical phrasing implied disrespect. This was double-acting or duality. Margaret resented the duplicity and felt (believed) that she was treated as unimportant, as unequal, as below Lillian's standard. Her cherished belief that she was as important as anybody else was offended. But in Recovery Margaret had learned that the supreme task of the nervous patient is to avoid symptoms and temper and that both symptoms and temper are easily aroused by the insistence on being treated as important. You know that, in our Recovery language, the sense of one's importance goes by the name of exceptionality or singularity. What we ask our patients to do is to cultivate the thought of averageness. If they do, they will not feel (believe to be) overly important. Then they will escape the "hurt feelings" of having their importance doubted, questioned, ridiculed and not taken seriously. Margaret expressed this Recovery philosophy beautifully when she reflected, "I was ready to come back with a sharp remark but...spotted this as temper and said to myself I am not going to work myself up...I have learned in Recovery to be average....Then...I thought nothing more of "my feelings." Her "feelings" were the belief in her importance, and when belief in averageness was substituted, calm and poise took the place of hurt feelings which is a misnomer for beliefs not shared.

DR. LOW'S COLUMN
BLINDSPOTTING AND SPOTLIGHTING

Agnes, on the Saturday panel, described a severe panic which she suffered about a year previous, just after she started her Recovery training. "One night I awakened from sleep and felt a jerking sensation in my head. The top of my head seemed to be slowly lifting into the air. The sensation kept repeating, and I soon had palpitations and heavy chest pressure. My breathing seemed to be cut off. I gasped and broke into a cold sweat, and I was so nauseated that I feared I would vomit before I could get out of bed. The room seemed to spin around me. I was sure I had a heart attack and woke my husband. He became alarmed and this alarmed me more. My husband rushed downstairs to call the family physician. The moment he stepped out of the room the thought came to me, 'now you are alone; now it will strike.' I screamed, and my scream made my husband rush back, and I begged him not to leave me alone. By this time my mother was up, and she stayed with me while my husband made the call to the physician. When he returned he told me that the physician couldn't come. He wanted me to take a sedative and to come to his office tomorrow. I was frantic and said, 'I won't be here tomorrow. What kind of doctor is he? A doctor who would not attend a sick and dying patient? Wait till I see him tomorrow. I am certainly going to give him a piece of my mind.' When my husband brought the tablets I refused to take them. I knew they were too strong for my weak heart and I might not awaken if I fell asleep. Finally I consented to take one tablet. Then I wrapped myself in a blanket, went down to the living room and sat in a big chair. They were not going to get rid of me that easily! I was going to sit up and fight off the effect of the sedative. But finally I fell asleep, and in the morning I was exhausted and felt all in for weeks." Agnes then mentioned that recently she had a similar panic at night. "My first impulse was to wake my husband. But I immediately knew that this was sabotage. So I decided not to work myself up but to do something objective, something entirely without emotion, as the doctor says in the article. I then looked at the reflection of the street light across the wall of my bedroom. I began to follow its pattern trying to figure out what it represented. I studied every line of it tracing all of them with my eyes. Soon I noticed I was breathing normally;

the palpitations, the nausea and sweats were gone in no time. Before long I was asleep again...."

Agnes was in panic. She felt it was a heart attack and death seemed imminent. The husband rushed to call the doctor which ought to have reassured Agnes but did not. Her reaction was, "Now you are alone, now it will strike." But it is not at all clear why death should contrive cunningly to strike its victim while it is alone. Agnes knew well, as everybody knows, that death has a conspicuous preference for doing its deathly business precisely in the presence of people, particularly in the presence of physicians, nurses or close relatives. If this is so, then, Agnes' statement was grossly contrary to common experience and common logic. Nor was this her only offense against the rules of logical thinking. When her husband returned from the unsuccessful call for the doctor, Agnes was understandably provoked by the physician's refusal to attend her in person. Then she delivered herself of utterances which cannot possibly be harmonized with even the shakiest logical rules. She said in reference to the physician's advice to visit his office on the day following, *"I won't be here tomorrow. What kind of doctor is he?...Wait till I see him tomorrow."* The logical contradiction is here glaring and startling. Agnes was convinced she would not live "tomorrow" but prepared herself to give the doctor "a piece of her mind" on that same "tomorrow." There are sundry other logical absurdities in Agnes' narrative, but I shall point merely to one more piece of twisted thinking. You will recall that Agnes feared that if she were left alone death would strike. But when the husband made her take the tablet she feared it might kill her and, to avert the danger of dying, she seated herself in a big chair in the living room, apart from husband and mother. You will admit that a logic which says that death strikes when you are *alone* and then proclaims that the best method of cheating death is to sit *alone* in a separate room is a bit wierd, strange and not a little delirious. All of this adds up to the realization that Agnes, endowed with a keen intelligence, managed succesfully to ignore logic when she was seized with a panic.

You remember that Agnes, while telling her story, smiled and laughed and at times broke into loud guffaws. We all shared her mirth responding with roars of laughter, which means that we noticed the absurdities in her account and refused to give them serious thought. Anybody in his right mind would laugh at such grotesque contradictions. Why, then, did Agnes fail to laugh on that night in which her brain produced those ridiculous fears? You might advance the theory that going through the frenzy of a panic she was "out of her mind", unable to use her reason. Unfortunately for this theory we have ample evidence that all through the panic Agnes reasoned with perfect logic about a doctor's duty to attend a dying patient, about his villainy of forsaking her, about her determination to call him to account the following morning. The reasoning was by no means realistic; it was romanticized, but its formal logic was flawless. She certainly demonstrated a good power of reasoning when she reflected that two tablets might kill her while one might be the proper dose; that the surest method of counteracting the deadening effect of a sedative was to stay awake. Obviously, Agnes had a good control over her reason but used it with an almost uncanny discrimination: She employed it correctly in one train of thought and incorrectly in another.

Reasoning is a tool, the tool of thinking. If a man, wielding a hammer (tool), drives all the nails correctly into the right half of a board but misses all or most of them in the left half, there must be something wrong with the man, not with the tool. Even if the man was intoxicated or panicky or fatigued, nevertheless, the perfect discrimination between the right and left side of the board shows that a pattern was followed and a choice made. The choice was to favor the right side of the board. That choice may have been unreflective, that is, not conscious. But it was a choice, guided by well contrived discrimnation. And choice and discrimination are functions of the Will. Did Agnes choose to make a faulty use of her reasoning power? Was it her Will to be absurd and illogical?

Whether an act is against reason and logic depends on the purpose it serves. If on a hot summer day I suffer from extreme heat it is good logic to seek comfort in the shade. If I do that I demonstrate that my realistic purpose was to secure relief in a cool spot. But if complaining of the "intolerable" heat, I step into the middle of the street exposing myself to the blazing sun; if all the while I yell at the top of my voice that I am boiling and sweating and roasting but do nothing to seek the shade; if I do all of this, then it is clear that my purpose was not to escape the heat but to attract attention, to be theatrical, to do something which other people would not do, to be exceptional, different and singular. All of this is called romanticism. To be romantic is not necessarily illogical. If it is your set purpose to indulge in silly heroics, a romantic imbecility will be a good means for realizing that purpose. It is absurd only if judged by the standard of realism. Realism demands sound reasoning, common sense and common logic. Romanticism requires nothing of the sort. Indeed, if it is to function and survive, it will have to shut off sense and logic. If you apply logic to a romanticist performance, you make it look ridiculous and kill the effect. In other words, it is good logic to shut off logical thinking if you want to relish your romantic absurdities. Realism thrives by logical reasoning, romanticism dies of it.

When Agnes threw her tantrum, she engaged in the romanticist game of staging a scene full of excitement, danger and drama. She played, with coarse and boisterous dramatization, the role of one threatened with death and destruction, posing as the helpless victim of a fatal emergency, all the while striking well calculated terror into the minds of husband and mother. A theatrical performance of this kind, being grotesque and ridiculous and utterly illogical, cannot be maintained convincingly unless the actor or actress blind themselves against the protest and cynical smile of logic and reason. Shut off reason and you can be a romanticist; employ reason and you must become a realist. When Agnes, a year after her gruesome midnight performance, had a similar experience with torturing symptoms, she turned realist, did a good piece of sound, logical thinking, and the developing tantrum was aborted in the space of seconds or minutes. Which method did she employ to eliminate romanticism and replace it with realism?

I do not know whether you are acquainted with the fact that the human eye is endowed with one spot in which vision does not function. It is called the blind spot, and an object on which this spot is focused is shut out from sight. That object is then *blindspotted*. The human eye has another tiny part which, when directed at an object, sees it with the clearest vision. That object is then *spotlighted*. The mind has a similar structure. Its function is to view things and experiences in order to discover their meanings. In this process the mind can, exactly as the physical eye, either blindspot or spotlight the things it views. If it turns its full attention on them, exploring them by means of reason and logic, then, it spotlights them and obtains their logical and realistic meaning. On the other hand, if the experience is painful or disturbing or unwelcome, it turns off attention, logic and reason, and the experience is blindspotted. You see here that what in Recovery we call "spotting" has two aspects. The one is blindspotting, the other spotlighting. If you want to indulge your silly romanto-intellectualisms, you will have to blind yourself to the realistic meanings of your experiences, that means, you will have to blind-spot them. If you desire to see clearly and realistically, you will have to turn the full light of logic and reason on them, that means, you will have to spotlight them. The romanto-intellectualist blindspots reality, the realist spotlights it. Agnes was given to blindspotting before she joined Recovery but became an accomplished spotlighter as a result of the training she received in our midst. What she demonstrated here with her telling the panel example was that Recovery has developed a singularly successful method of converting as confirmed a romanto-intellectualist as Agnes used to be, into a logic-wielding realist as she is now. The substance of the method is to train patients to scrap their blind-spotting and to practice spotlighting with regard to experiences, particularly with regard to symptoms and temper.

DR. LOW'S COLUMN
TOTAL PERSONALITY AND TOTAL SITUATION

Beatrice, on the Saturday panel, reported the following experience: "My husband," she said, "had the habit of going out for cigarettes and staying several hours. This used to lead to temper outbursts on my part. I wanted him to admit he was wrong to leave me alone, and I wanted him to say he was sorry. This always ended in an argument which I never won. I spent many years trying to change him and making him admit he was doing me a great injustice. In Recovery I learned that environment could be put miles away from you, and if I couldn't change my husband I would have to change my attitude towards him. This meant controlling my speech muscles and doing away with arguments. But when I couldn't express my feelings I felt as though I would burst. Nevertheless, I kept my mouth shut and there were less and less arguments. One night my husband announced he was going out for cigarettes and he would be right back. This time I made up my mind to say nothing, and I wasn't going to be angry. So I prepared myself for bed, taking my Recovery literature with me. After I finished reading I dozed off to sleep when I heard him come into the house. When he entered our bedroom I greeted him but said nothing else. He looked surprised, obviously expecting me to be angry. He commented that it was rather late and I agreed with him. I told him then to get in bed as I had to get up early in the morning. He asked, 'Don't you want to know where I have been?' I said it wasn't necessary and he could tell me in the morning. I closed my eyes but when I didn't hear him moving around the room I looked up, and there he was standing by my bed staring at me. I asked him what was wrong and he said, 'I am just looking to see if there isn't a strange woman in my bed.' I assured him it wasn't a strange but a changed woman. . . . We are both happy about the change, and the change in me has even brought about a change in him. Now when he goes out he is always back in a very short time."

Beatrice spent many futile years trying desperately to change her husband, Bill, but finally decided to change herself instead. The result was that she was a changed wife and he a changed husband. Family life was reorganized and the ailing marital situation restored to health. But Beatrice was only one partner to the

27

marital situation. The other partner was Bill. How is it that the total marital situation changed when one of the partners only mended her ways? There is nothing in the record to indicate that Bill made any effort to reform his behavior. Beatrice specifically states that "the change in me has even brought about a change in him." If this is so, then, a total situation was corrected when one part of it only was repaired.

Beatrice claims she changed her "Self." Which Self does she refer to? She certainly did not reshape and recreate her *physical Self*, not her stomach, lungs, face, legs and arms. I can state with equal assurance that she did not effect a change in her *psychological Self*. She did not alter her mode of remembering, her attention and concentration, her manner of receiving impressions, her logic and reasoning power. What she must have made over when she changed was her *sociological Self*, that Self which reacts to and manages group life, and may be properly called the group Self. And the group Self is the domain of the personality. We conclude that the change which Beatrice effected concerned her personality. And, since the change was of a radical nature, thorough and enduring and apparently final, we must assume that the total of her personality was changed. Remarkably, the radical reorganization of her *total personality* produced an equally thorough and enduring and apparently final reconditioning of the *total situation* of her married life.

What is meant by total personality? What by total situation? In a given situation an individual may act in two ways: Either as a single, isolated person driven by subjective impulses, or as a personality guided by the commonly accepted standards and values of the group. If, as an unmarried person, you are alone at home and have the impulse to eat a dish of food, there is no group rule to govern your decision. You may, at will, yield to the impulse or hold it down. Suppose, however, you are a father. As such you belong to the group of your family. The rules of a well-ordered family life provide that meals be taken jointly by the entire group. Eating alone would run counter to the needs and interests of the common family purpose. Being guided by the standards of family life you will curb your hunger and suppress the impulse to eat apart from the other members of the group. You will now understand that the chief characteristic of a personality is that individualistic impulses are sacrificed to group needs.

In exercising the paternal functions of his personality a father encounters many difficulties. The plumbing goes wrong and the roof develops a leak; and expenses pile up and business declines; and the wife clamors for new furniture, and the children neglect the chores and mess up the house. All of this creates annoyance and irritation, perhaps disgust and a sense of helplessness. The frustration mobilizes impulses: To give up the effort altogether, to seek distraction outside the home, to release temper outbursts. Each time the father yields to his impulses, he acts as an *unrestrained person* relinquishing the title to being a *self-controlled personality*. The totality of his life is then broken up into various segments. In some segments of his behavior he is still a disciplined personality, in others he conducts himself as an erratic, impulsive, fickle person. If this happens, the father has changed from a total to a *segmented personality*. Behavior is then no longer unifed and dominated by the standards and values of the group purpose but capriciously swaying between the group goals of the personality and the individualistic impulses of the person.

Prior to her Recovery training, Beatrice was clearly a segmental personality. As such she behaved as most people do: Sometimes her conduct was directed by the impulses of the individualistic person, at other times by the policies and principles of the group personality. From what we know about Beatrice we may safely assume that in the majority of the situations the group personality scored over the individualistic person and that most of her actions were governed by rules and standards. On many occasions she experienced an "intolerable" fatigue but the impulse to neglect the household duties was promptly suppressed, and the obligations of mother and wife were discharged in spite of an overwhelming desire to escape them. Or, she felt a numbness in the extremities, "as if the legs were a mass of stone," but the house was cleaned without hesitation, the furniture was dusted with dispatch, and the meals prepared on schedule. Many a time she was "just a bundle of nerves, edgy and jumpy" until she "felt like bursting;" nevertheless, temper was usually or frequently controlled when she dealt with her little daughter. Moreover—and this is greatly to Beatrice's credit—she unfailingly catered to the comfort of her husband, ignoring his "impossible" behavior and her "just" grievances. In all of this she controlled the impulses of her person and acted as a group personality. But in many other situations she was ruled by the impact of personal urges and desire, of subjective preferences and resentments. These were the numerous occasions in which she staged violent tantrums, when she insisted that her husband "admit he was wrong," when she "wanted him to say he was sorry" and demanded of him a formal confession that he did her "a great injustice." In those pre-Recovery days, her personality was currently invaded and sidetracked by the various segments of her person. It was segmental instead of total.

Of course, there is not, nor can there be, an absolutely total personality. A person who would always behave strictly in accord with group standards would have a record of perfection and cease to be a healthy, average human being. An absolutely total personality of this type would be equipped with a sublime character, with impeccable habits, with ethereal feelings and divine motives. He would be a wizard, hero, saint and angel, all combined. An individual of this stamp would be undesirable even if possible. Be certain that when Beatrice grew to be a total personality, her totality was relative and limited and, in a sense, patchy. What really happened after her change of attitude was that her behavior as wife and mother, perhaps also as friend and neighbor, became less and less segmental and more and more total. She acquired a good measure of total patterns but happily retained an equally good measure of natural averageness and human imperfection.

Beatrice acquired the status of a relatively total personality through the training she received in Recovery. But her husband, Bill, did not pass through the discipline of the Recovery techniques. To my knowledge he never came to our meetings. I met him once on the occasion of a lawn party, and I can assure you that he was not run through any course of training there. Yet, the transformation wrought in Beatrice, from an individualistic person to a total personality, somehow carried over to him. When she changed, he changed; when she dropped her antagonism and began practicing cooperation, he followed in the same track; she discarded her temper, and he turned congenial and considerate. In other words, one partner changed her attitude, and the *total marital situation* assumed a new aspect. This sounds like miracle and mystery but is nothing of the kind. To the contrary, it is precisely what should and could be expected of any *life situation* as contrasted with a purely *mechanical situation*. In a mechanical situation, let me say in the situation of an automobile, you may inflate one tire, and the air content of the other tires will not at all be affected. A life situation reacts in an entirely different fashion. It is composed of living human beings who form a group either of cooperating partners or antagonistic partisans. As partners they work together creating peace, good will and mutual understanding. As partisans they act at cross-purpose creating dissension, ill will and misunderstanding. But whether partners or partisans, they influence one another. If the one member of the team changes, the other is affected. Prior to her Recovery training, Beatrice was an opposing partisan to her husband. In our language, she acted on Bill with temper. There was a running domestic battle in which tempers clashed continuously. In this family warfare, whenever Beatrice struck out against Bill she provoked his temper, and he struck back at her. In this way, her temper abetted and activated his. After she learned to curb her own temperamental impulses, she approached her husband with calm, poise and a disarming sense of humor. There was no striking out on her part, hence, no striking back on his part. The total marital situation changed from aggression to cooperation when the one partner converted her segmental personality into a total personality.

The story told by Beatrice carries a vital lesson for all my patients. When I tell them that it is temper which upsets their nervous system; that in order to get well and keep well their tempers will have to be curbed; when I tell them these commonplace truths, their standard reply is that it is not their own temper which needs the curbing but that of their husband, wife, mother or daughter. I grant that the members of the family display abundant temper in dealing with the patient. But it is he who suffers and not they; it is his nervous system which requires care, not theirs. The family is the patient's main environment. It represents the most important total situation in which he is placed. That it needs a change and that its temperamental charge must be reduced cannot be denied. But what my patients must learn is the lesson which Beatrice phrased in words, both beautiful and forceful, when she said that in Recovery she was made to realize "that environment could be put miles away from you, and that if I couldn't change my husband I would have to change my attitude towards him." Any of my patients could change his or her attitude. I shall add that all of them could effect that radical change, thorough and enduring, which Beatrice produced in her marital life. A radical change of this kind establishes a total situation in which the one partner ceases fighting and forces the other to lay down his weapons because there is no opponent left to lash out against. The "cease fire" order is bound to be followed by a temporary truce and finally by a lasting peace. And under conditions of a sustained peace, both partners will be in a position to develop their total personalities by eliminating from them the temperamental segment which disturbs totality of behavior and creates segmentalism of reaction. If this comes to pass the patient will have cured his nerves through Self-Help. The abiding value of the example presented by Beatrice is that Self-Help as practiced in Recovery is not merely a vague and shadowy theory but a concrete and living reality provided the practicing is done by as valiant and resolute a patient as Beatrice.

DR. LOW'S COLUMN
EXPECTATIONS AND DISAPPOINTMENTS

At a recent panel discussion, Helen S. reported that several weeks ago she was invited to a friend's home. A number of her friends were present. The conversation turned to a woman in the neighborhood who, suffering from a nervous ailment, was highly suggestible to the point where if an illness was mentioned she "had it." The hostess remarked, "That is nothing unusual. Nervous people have weak minds." Helen then contrasted her reaction on that occasion with what would have happened had a statement of this kind been passed in her presence at the time when she had not yet received her Recovery training. "At that time," she said, "the slightest reference to the mind or anything mental made me tense all over the body, especially my head. I would have become dizzy, and my head pressure would have been with me for days. Worst of all, I would have been convinced that that was precisely what was wrong with me: I was weak-minded. If I hadn't lost my mind already I was surely on the way and would eventually lose it. Of course, the more I thought of it the more severe was my tenseness, and the greater the tenseness the stronger the conviction. A vicious cycle and a panic would follow and last for days and weeks. This time I first felt the impulse to say, 'Anna, I am nervous. How can you say I am weak-minded?' But I checked the impulse and just smiled and let it go at that...." At the same panel Ann M. reported that one day recently she dropped in at a neighborhood grocery store where she currently cashes her paychecks. This time she had two checks instead of one. The cashier said in a gruff tone of voice, "I cannot cash two checks, and remember, lady, I am not your banker." Ann was flushed and embarrassed, she said, "but I instantly spotted my feelings as unimportant and stopped the angry reply which I was ready to make. I laughed at myself and my sense of importance...."

Helen and Ann were exposed to remarks, the one by her hostess, the other by a store employee, and both were "struck" by the statements as if they had received a body blow. Clearly, if the remarks "struck," they were not expected. What Helen did expect was that the word "mind" and "mental" should not be used in her presence. And Ann expected that a simple request should be granted, and if a refusal was offered, it should be couched in courteous language. When the expectations did not come true, when they did not find fulfillment, Helen and Ann were "struck" by a sense of frustration. Which brings us face to face with the problems of fulfillment and frustration. And the question arises: What do people generally expect? Which expectations are likely to bring fulfillment, which frustration?

To have expectations means to look ahead into the future. You expect a friend to visit you, a letter to arrive, the daily newspaper to be handy for your breakfast, the evening meal to be ready on time; or you expect your daughter to be married or your son to pass his examination. All these events can only take place at some future date. If you think of making a go of your business your thought is, of course, directed toward the future. And if you crave security or hope for advancement or wish for success, all of these are expectations which point to the future. The future is that part of your life for which you strive and labor and pray. It is the object of your ambition and aspiration, the goal of your hopes and dreams; in short, it is your life. You may say that life is what you expect of the future. Whether your future will be one of fulfillment or of frustration depends on the manner in which you manage your expectations.

Expectations are of two kinds: hope or fear. Your daughter is to be married. If the future son-in-law is a person of character and pleasing qualities, your expectation is in the nature of a hope; if you have conceived a dislike for him, your expectation will be that of fear. Suppose he is a man of substance, loved by your daughter and respected by your husband. But for some unexplainable reason you have formed an intense antipathy towards him. In that event, your fearful expectation was not produced by the actions and qualities of your prospective son-in-law but was born and hatched inside you and by you. Presumably you have formed an expectation, unbeknown to yourself, that your daughter must not marry at all, that she should belong to you exclusively and grant no share of her existence to anybody except you. An expectation of this kind is called possessiveness. It is an extreme personal attitude, backed neither by common sense nor by commonly accepted standards. It is entirely a creation of your own, born of your grotesque vanity which makes you think that you are an exceptional mother and your child an exceptional daughter and that the exceptional care, tenderness and understanding which your daughter requires can be supplied by you only. If now your daughter decides to go through with her marriage plans, your expectations are frustrated, and you are disappointed. The disappointment is due to the fact that you appointed yourself as a possessive person, a person who has an exceptional and exclusive claim on the affection and life of your daughter. This claim is self-appointed. If it is thwarted by your daughter's decision, the resulting frustration is of your own making. You cannot blame your daughter for wanting to be married. Her role as a bride, as a prospective mother and wife was appointed for her by common practice and common standards. In other words, her expectation of joining a husband is *group-appointed*. Your expectation of keeping the daughter to yourself is *self-appointed*. If your self-appointed expectations meet with frustration and are denied fulfillment, the ensuing disappointment is self-induced, and the responsibility for the defeat is entirely yours. The popular saying, "As you make your bed so will you lie in it," refers precisely to this matter of self-appointed expectations leading to self-induced frustrations.

Neither Helen nor Ann nor any of my charges have appointed for themselves the role of being a nervous patient. If their original ailment caused them untold suffering, the responsibility was not theirs. They had a weak nervous system, it is true. But the weakness was due to their constitution, and their constitution was an inheritance, given them by destiny and fate. We conclude that, originally, their nervous illness was *fate-appointed*, not self-appointed. However, after they contracted their nervous condition, they formed extreme and grotesque expectations. These were self-appointed, and the subsequent agonies and frustrations were decidedly self-created. Consider the case of Helen. When she first came to see me she had a record of almost thirty years of more or less continuous suffering. During all this time she entertained the fear that her mind was in the process of disintegrating. This was an expectation, self-made and self-conceived. Moreover, when I tried to disabuse her of the absurd idea (expectation) that her mind was about to collapse, she used all her energy to refute my statement. Her theory of impending disaster was defended with the strength of a deep and stubborn conviction. Ann who had a shorter career of nervous disturbance performed in a similar manner. She resisted my positive suggestions with force clinging to her negative suggestions with a wild tenacity which would have been a credit to a person fighting for a noble purpose. Both, of course, assumed and insisted that they were beyond hope, that they were the only ones afflicted with a condition of this kind. And if theirs was the "only case" how could they ever expect to find a doctor who knew its nature and could cure "a case like this"? Steeped in a philosophy of gloom, as they were, it was only natural that they should ask the fatal question: How long can a human body go through these agonies without collapsing? To you who are familiar with my writings, it will be clear by now that these lugubrious, hope-excluding expectations are nothing but the three basic fears which I have described: the fears of physical collapse, mental collapse and permanent handicap. As such they were self-made diagnoses, hotly defended, as self-acquired property usually is, and fought for with savage and ferocious arguments. The diagnoses were what we call the process of self-diagnosing, a self-appointed expectation of doleful happenings, or a self-chosen diagnostic defeatism. (About the meaning of the three basic fears see "Mental Health Through Will-Training," Concise Outline.)

In the course of time Helen and Ann developed, as all my patients do, all manner of other expectations. They expected everybody to listen patiently and appreciatively to their never-ending complaints. They expected the physician to perform miracles of healing and to secure for them instant and lasting relief. They had a mysterious and fantastic expectation that there was a "physical cause" to their trouble and spent numbers of years and small fortunes wandering from specialist to specialist in a desperate search for that mythical "cause." Bleak disappointment was invariably the painful result of these self-appointed expectations. Meeting with an unbroken chain of cumulative disappointments, they finally reached the point when they expected to be disappointed and decided that nobody cared for them, that nobody understood, respected or wanted them. Their extravagant expectations created for them a situation in which they felt forsaken, isolated, rejected, stigmatized. In the case of Helen, the fear of being stigmatized made her shudder when the words "mind" or "mental" were merely mentioned, even if they did not at all refer to her. With Ann, the thought of not being wanted or respected threw her into a flush and embarrassment when a trivial request of hers was not duly honored or when a mild criticism was directed against her. The passion for continuous self-appointments had created a condition of sustained disappointment.

If I state that the agonies of my patients are largely "self-induced," "self-made" and "self-created," I do not wish to imply that nervous sufferers plan their symptoms deliberately, or that their panics and vicious cycles are consciously contrived and manufactured. What I mean to convey to you is that these reactions, if unduly prolonged, are produced by them intuitively. (About intuitive and discursive thinking see "Mental Health," Part IV, Ch. 7.) Your self-appointed expectations are intuitive, of course. They are decidedly not discursive. An example will give you an illustration how the intuitive process works: A patient told me some time ago that, on weekdays, he "simply can't" get out of bed before 10 AM and sometimes hugs the bed till early afternoon. "Isn't it funny," he continued "that on Sundays I jump out of bed without any trouble?" I had no difficulty explaining this seeming paradox. The man is suffering from a depression which means that planning, making decisions and giving instructions are an ordeal to him. If he went to his office he would have to do the planning, deciding and instructing which was so distasteful to him. In order to escape the ordeal he spent the morning hours in bed, shunning the painful routine of the office. On Sundays, the office was closed, and there was no ordeal to be guarded against. Hence, he was able to arise at an early hour "without any trouble." In this case, my patient, a successful business man, carried out in his brain without being aware of it (intuitively), the following complex train of thought: "I *hate* the office routine...I *wish* I could escape it...If I *decide* to stay in bed I shall *spare myself* a great deal of distress...I do not *have to* manage the office on Sundays...on Sundays I *can* get up early." He hated and wished and decided and knew what he had to do on some days and could do on other days, and all these involved thought processes were manipulated without any conscious deliberation. They were thought about intuitively. When I turned the full light of my conscious logic on the man's reaction I was able to discourse freely about his conduct which was "funny" to him but did not puzzle me at all. Since I discoursed with him in clear awareness of the hidden meaning of his behavior, my thoughts were discursive, not intuitive. After I revealed to the patient the discursive significance of his action, his "funny" hatreds and wishes and plans were spotted as intuitively self-induced, self-made and self-created. Then he was trained, not merely taught, to practice our spotting techniques himself, to exercise proper muscle control and to stop his not at all "funny" habits.

I hope you will now understand that your self-appointed expectations are intuitive productions of your brain, self-induced and self-created. Being pushed back into the background of your consciousness, they are not known to you. You will also understand that the method of getting rid of your harmful and healthwrecking expectations is the proper use of our spotting techniques. What must be spotted is the intuitive meaning of your self-appointments. If your spotting is done correctly, after due Recovery training, you will be able to use your conscious Will for the purpose of saying a resounding "No" to your intuitive strivings and stop them effectively through control of muscles. That's what Helen and Ann did after they had received their training in Recovery.

DR. LOW'S COLUMN
SELF-SPOTTING AND FOREIGN SPOTTING

Florence reported on the Saturday panel that some time ago her husband decided to wax the floor. He asked her to stop at the hardware store for the purpose of renting an electric waxer. "I told him I didn't think we should rent the waxer because they charged two dollars an hour as rental. 'What?' said my husband, 'Two dollars an hour? That sounds like highway robbery. Are you sure you are right?' I spoke right up and said, 'I know I am right. I read it in the paper yesterday and still have the ad.' He asked me to show it to him, and I didn't like that and said, 'Yesterday we discussed in Recovery the article "The Vanity of Knowing Better." You should have been there.' But I went for the ad, and when I looked at it, it read, 'Waxer, two dollars a day.' I was stunned. Here I had started an argument and tried to prove to my husband that the cost was two dollars an hour when it was only two dollars a day. What irked me most was that it was I who had shown the Vanity of Knowing Better and had thrown it up to him...." Florence then described how she instantly had a severe pressure at the top of her head, pain in the eyes and blurred vision. But she spotted it promptly as the anger at having made a mistake, and instead of continuing her temperamental raving, she laughed at her stupid behavior and knew it was an average stupidity. She admitted the mistake and apologized for her Vanity of Knowing Better. The spotting disposed of her symptoms in a short time.

In the example which Florence mentioned on the panel, the point at issue was whether the two-dollar rental for an electric waxer was computed on an hourly or daily basis. It would have been easy for Florence to spot this as a minor difference of opinion, too paltry to get excited over it. Instead, she "spoke right up," exclaiming wildly and petulantly, "I know I am right." There can be no doubt that at that moment she had at her command the Recovery principle that there is no judge to decide who is right or wrong in matters domestic. Why did she neglect to recall that maxim so well known to her? In view of her intensive training and extensive practice, it should have been easy for her to realize that her temperamental explosion was nothing but a silly claim to exceptional knowledge, a romanto-intellectualist boast of "knowing better." When she voiced the defiant phrase, "I know

I am right," why did it not occur to her in a flash that this was the pretense of intellectual superiority, worse yet, a grab for domination and mastery? When her husband asked her to show him the ad she "didn't like that." This was a naive admission that, in her opinion, the husband had no "right" to question the correctness of her assumptions. Why did she neglect to spot this as plain vanity and rank individualism? Why did she at this moment fail to remember the numerous distinctions she had learned in Recovery about "partnership and partisanship," "sovereignty and fellowship," "averageness and exceptionality," "group-mindedness and self-mindedness?" Why did she forget that "feelings are not facts?" These and a host of other concise formulations would have been certain to stop her dizzy flight to romanto-intellectualist heights and could have been depended on to bring her back to the solid ground of sober realistic thinking. Summing up, I shall ask: Why did Florence, one of our master spotters, "forget" to employ her spotting skills when, in a fit of temper, she gave way to a burst of hysteria? Why did she ignore and jeopardize the vital needs of health and home?

That Florence had indeed acquired a most creditable degree of spotting facility she demonstrated convincingly when, casting a glance at the ad, she became aware of her mistake. She felt "stunned," she says. It was a stunning blow to her self-respect and sense of decency when it dawned on her that she had accused her husband of the "Vanity of Knowing Better" at the very moment when she indulged precisely that vanity herself. She displayed a most exquisite expertness in self-spotting when, struck by a bout of symptoms, she judged them correctly as "the anger at having made a mistake." Or, when she disposed of her self-disgust by laughing at her own stupidity and "knew it was an average stupidity." That her method of spotting was of a high-grade quality was proved when her symptoms vanished in a short time. If she was an expert spotter in one instance, with her symptoms, why was she so grievously deficient in the other instance, with her temper? And the more general and more crucial question arises: Why are my patients in such haste to forget so readily what they have learned so wearily? Is spotting difficult to learn? Is it easy to forget?

There is no mystery to the spotting performance. Pre-school children have, on an average, no difficulty practicing the art to perfection in the field of primitive logic, mathematics and grammar. Let a child of this age state inadvertently that Paul is *strongest than* John, and not a second will pass before the tot will correct to *stronger than*. Let him blurt out the sentence, "I went to the circus *next week*," and he will promptly recognize the mistake, saying "I meant *last week*." He will similarly spot and correct his error when, in childish pride, he exclaims that he got *two* pieces of candy and ate all *three* of them. I doubt whether any group of parents have ever made an effort to teach their children how to practice the art of spotting. I presume to doubt also whether there are many parents who could supply the required instruction. Moreover, if there were such parents their effort would be needlessly wasted because the children could not possibly grasp the implied principle. If this is so, we must conclude that children practice their spotting without ever being taught the practice. In other words, spotting is as easy as the proverbial "child's play." It is not necessary to acquire it because it is born with you. You come by it naturally, without any special training. And if it can be manipulated with ease by children, why is it so difficult for my patients to master it? And if a patient such as Florence has actually achieved spotting mastery, why is she likely to "forget" it or lose it in a fit of temper?

You may call it unfair to compare the primitive spotting function of infants to the complex performance expected of adult persons. Infantile spotting, you will argue, is perhaps an inherited and inborn faculty. If it is, well, it may be "as easy as a child's play." But adult spotting, assuredly, calls for training. Why, then, suspect a bungling spotter of being incurably addicted to romanto-intellectualism? Would lack of training not be a fairer explanation? This appeal to my sense of fairness lacks force in my particular case because I cannot possibly be accused of having given my patients insufficient training in spotting. The argument will lose ground completely if you will take the trouble to observe the behavior of ordinary people under ordinary circumstances, quite apart from temperamental impulsiveness and disturbing symptoms. You will then notice that the average person, largely untrained, does a remarkably good job, in conversation or debate, spotting the reactions of others (of others only), uncovering with ease and exposing with glee (in the other fellow) inconsistencies and contradictions, errors of judgment and logical fallacies, poor

manners and tactless utterances, unseemly gestures and com-
promising habits. Note, however, how at the very moment when
he spotlights masterfully the misbehavior of others he may be
guilty of similar misconduct himself. This he "forgets" to
spotlight. Instead, he blindspots it. (About Spotlighting and
Blindspotting see Recovery News, August 1950.) Do you grasp the
underlying principle? Adult persons have their spotting techniques at their fingers' tips and apply them expertly when the
other fellow is involved. They are past masters in the field of *foreign spotting*. In the field of *self-spotting* they usually fail miser-
ably. Is it logical to assume that all these dexterous spotters were
trained in foreign spotting only? Is it possible that they received
special courses in nothing else but fault-finding, cavilling and
acrimonious criticism? The only plausible explanation, it would
appear, is that the art of spotting is inborn, apart from instruction
and training, but is put into practice only when the proper incentive is operating. Everybody, even a child, spots correctly and
eagerly in matters of elementary logic, mathematics and grammar.
The incentive here is to preserve one's intellectual reputation.
Likewise, everybody is ready and frequently itching to spot the erroneous thought and faulty action of other persons. The incentive
is here to display superior intelligence by exposing others as lacking it. There is no such incentive to expose, that is, to spot one's
own inadequacies of thought and action. Expressing it otherwise:
Foreign spotting is pleasure and is engaged in with gusto. Self-
spotting is or may be painful and is graciously dispensed with.

Foreign spotting is important for the understanding of the
desires, feelings and motives of your friends and enemies. I mentioned its significance in conversation and debate. It is of value, of
course, to anybody who is engaged in the task of instructing or
guiding or somehow influencing people. It is indispensable to
parents, teachers, ministers, statesmen, buyers, sellers, in short, to
anyone who acts or works in close contact with other persons. After
thus underscoring its universal and supreme importance, I shall
now confess that I ignore it almost completely in the training
which I give my patients. The reason is not far to seek. My duty is
to rid my patients of their suffering. What they suffer from
predominantly are their symptoms and their tempers. No amount
of instruction in the art of understanding people will contribute
materially to the successful management of sensations or to the ef-

fective control of tempers. What my patients must concentrate on is self-spotting. From what I know about Florence I doubt whether her understanding of the desires, feelings and motives of others was of any conspicuous depth or breadth. It was and still is of average quality, sufficient to secure her against clashes with neighbors and friends but hardly adequate to protect her against the wily tricks of a slick salesman. To put it differently: Foreign spotting is practiced by my patients with no less nor more skill than that possessed by the average individual. More than this they do not need. Self-spotting is in a different category. The average individual knows little of it nor is he in urgent need of it for successful performance in his daily round. Free from panics and vicious cycles he will tend more or less efficiently to the routine of home and job, spotting or no spotting. Not so my patients. They may dispense with a great amount of foreign spotting without suffering consequences. But if they are to escape the torture of symptoms, they will have to acquire expertness in the art of self-spotting. Moreover, if the method is to be effective it will have to catch the symptom at the very moment when it starts to rumble and the temperamental disturbance just when it begins to stir. Both must be caught on the wing, as it were, before either has had a chance to be "worked up" into paroxysms of agonies. You may remember that I have given the name of trigger-spotting to this requirement for instant intervention. Florence learned in Recovery how to trigger-spot her symptoms to the point where she is practically free from them. This remarkable degree of mastery she obtained through persistent effort at self-control and self-scrutiny, that is, through untiring self-spotting. She spots her symptoms the very minute they rise to consciousness. More than that, she spots them correctly as "merely nervous," as "distressing but not dangerous," in other words, she has learned to fit her spot diagnosis into the pattern of the field diagnosis which I gave her on the occasion of the first examination. What she will have to do is to perform the same feat of trigger-spotting in the matter of temper. (About Spot Diagnosis and Field Diagnosis, see "Mental Health Through Will Training," Part III, Ch. 7.)

1. *Identifying Versus Interpretive Diagnoses*

Out in front of you stands a man. You look at him and know who he is. This knowledge you obtained through your eyes, that is, through visual perception. The man speaks to you, and you understand his language through your ears, that is, through auditory perception. After receiving knowledge of him through eyes and ears, you identify him as a friend of yours. The man is outside of you, in your external environment. You may conclude that knowledge of external environment comes to you through *sense perception.*

When you saw the man and heard his voice and then concluded that he was your friend you made a diagnosis. He could have been nothing more than a casual acquaintance or a perfect stranger, perhaps an enemy, but you identified or classified him as a friend. Every identification or classification is a diagnosis, a so-called *identifying or classificatory diagnosis.* Identifying diagnoses, made through the senses in external environment, require no special training. They certainly require no spotting efficiency. Anyone who is not mentally deranged can diagnose correctly the identity of persons or objects presented to him in external environment.

There are no persons or palpable objects to be identified or diagnosed within you, in your internal environment. What you observe there are functions and processes, the functions of thinking and feeling and the processes of sensations and impulses.

If you want to identify and diagnose them you will have to make use of your inner perception which we call *introspection.* Again, anyone not mentally deranged can identify or diagnose a given sensation as pain or dizziness, a given fear as the dread of mental collapse, or a given impulse as the urge to harm the baby. You will now understand that identifying diagnoses call for nothing more than average skill of outer perception and inner introspection. It ought to be clear to you then, that it is easy to identify or diagnose what environment is. The difficulty begins when you want to know, not what environment is but what it *means.* Is the man in front of you a genuine friend or is he pretending?

Does the pain mean danger or security? Is the fear sentimental or realistic? Is the impulse out of control or manageable? This is no mere outer and inner perception but *interpretation*. The average person can perceive properly which means that he is competent to make a correct identifying diagnosis. But an accurate interpretation which furnishes the *interpretive diagnosis* calls for training by a leader. The patient who perceives a symptom and rushes to supply his own interpretive diagnosis sabotages the authority and leadership of his physician. He is almost certain to misinterpret his condition and, through the wrong interpretation, deceive himself into impulsive and harmful action. Self-diagnosing is self-deceiving, if the diagnosis is interpretive.

2. *Muscular and Mental Habits*

Suffering can either be reported objectively or complained about subjectively. If the patient says, "In the morning I feel tired. I stay in bed and hate to get up," that is a plain objective report of what is felt or done. But if he says, "In the morning my body feels dead, I feel like in a grave," that is a subjective emotional exclamation, not of what the patient experiences but what he diagnoses. In using the words "death" and "grave" the complainer makes the diagnosis of a serious condition difficult to cure. This is defeatism. It breeds a belief of hopelessness and a sense of insecurity, a fear of doom and disaster. Since the complaining is done through the muscles (of speech) it is a muscular act. Since the defeatism is an attitude of the mind it is a mental act. If persisted in for months and years, both the muscular and mental acts harden into set habits resistive to change. In time, a vicious cycle establishes itself between the musular and mental habit. The more complaining is practiced the deeper grows the defeatism. The deeper the defeatism the more insistent the complaining. Stop the muscular habit of complaining, and you will put an end to the mental habit of defeatism.

3. *Self-Endorsement and Predisposition*

While driving my car I carry out thousands of discrete part-acts in a brief space of time. The right leg presses against the pedal, then steps on the brake. The left leg pushes in the clutch. The arms meanwhile direct the steering wheel. The eyes glance across the scene. Each of these part-acts comprises a number of self-repeating performances. I not only manipulate the steering wheel but keep manipulating it. I let it glide through my hands, or jerk it suddenly to the side, shift and turn it continuously. In the same manner, the brake, clutch, gears and eyes are kept adjusting in frequent sequences. In each of these thousands of part-acts I take the position, for instance, that my manner of turning the wheel is correct, that I turned it exactly as required. This is the position of self-approval and self-endorsement. A person who endorses himself feels secure. Or, a person who feels secure has endorsed himself. Self-endorsement is so important because the sense of security which it produces makes for sure and determined action. With proper self-endorsement, all the part-acts are released with the certain knowledge that I know how to drive, that I can be trusted to proceed correctly, that if I make a mistake it is likely to be a trifling matter. In order to take positions of security in each single part-act, I must have the *disposition* to think of myself as a trustworthy person in general and as a safe driver in particular. In addition, I must of course be able to think of my car as a dependable vehicle. The one disposition to feel secure in the total act of driving creates the countless positions of security with which I carry out the numerous part-acts of steering, braking, etc. Feeling secure in the total act enables me to go about each part-act with a sense of firmness and safety. But let me set out on my ride shortly after having suffered a shock to my self-esteem. Suppose I have discovered that I am guilty of a damaging tactlessness or of a grievous exhibit of poor judgement or of a gross neglect of duty. Suppose further that such moments of self-blame are common in my life, that I am frequently disposed to view myself with distrust, that the dispositions to distrust myself have turned into settled habits. I may then approach all or most of my acts, total or part, with a *predisposition* of insecurity. I will now doubt my general efficiency and dependability and will extend the general verdict of untrustworthiness to myself as driver. Thus predisposed to rate myself as a poor driver, my positions for each part-act (of pedalling, steering, gear-shifting, etc.) will lack the sense of safety, accuracy and precision. The predisposition to think in terms of

46

insecurity will lower my dispositions for total acts and render insecure my positions taken in part-acts. What you can learn from this example is that it is futile to watch and supervise narrow positions or even broad dispositions. What you must do instead is to train your most comprehensive predispositions to assume the quality of security. Your leading and supreme predisposition is your philosophy of life which you know is either realistic or sentimental. With a realistic philosophy to guide your actions you will feel average and will not be haunted by the fear of making mistakes. Your behavior will be cautious not fearful, firm not bold, balanced not vacillating. Conversely, if a sentimental philosophy directs your conduct you will feel exceptional (romanticist or intellectualist), and the perpetual dread of not reaching perfection will make you feel inadequate, unreliable, inefficient. You will be restless, apprenhensive, fitful, distrusting yourself. In order to acquire a philosophy of realism and averageness you will have to engage in a ceaseless process of spotting your positions and dispositions, an art which you learn in Recovery. What Recovery teaches you, through its philosophy of averageness, is to endorse your successes and to refrain from condemning your failures. An attitude of this kind permits you to accumulate a vast fund of self-endorsement which is made to flow in a running stream from your leading predisposition (philosophy) down to your dispositions for total acts, finally to seep through to each separate position taken in every single part-act.

4. Bodily Tools and Mental Attitudes

Every act has a goal which must be aimed at with the proper means or tools. If your present goal is to write a letter to a friend, the proper tools to use are letterhead, envelope and pen, a solid table and a suitable source of light. These are the *physical tools*. If the letter is meant to show a firm grasp of the theme and a good measure of warmth and feeling, you will do well to put yourself in the right mood and to be in fair command of memory, logic, language and style. These are the *mental tools*. But even with the best physical and mental tools you may fail at the job of writing if fear intervenes, if you think you are incompetent and feel insecure. This is your *mental attitude*. If the latter is that of self-distrust, it will create self-consciousness and will deprive you of the spontaneity which is needed for precise aiming.

The organs of the body are tools. Heart, lungs, stomach and others are physical tools employed in the service of bodily functions. Thoughts, feelings, impulses and others are mental tools employed in the service of psychological behavior. Whether they will work properly and will aim correctly at their goals will depend on your mental attitude. If the latter is that of self distrust you will be suspicious of your tools (of digestion, circulation, impulses, feelings, etc.) The greater will be your distrust of the organs, the more disturbed will be their functions. The more their functions will suffer, the more intense will be the symptoms. And all of it will be the direct outcome of your faulty mental attitude of self-distrust.

If, after due examination, I tell a patient that his is a nervous ailment, the implication is that his physical and mental tools are in good condition and that the only thing wrong with him is his mental attitude of self-distrust. In Recovery he is instructed that his warped attitude is caused by a distorted, unrealistic philosophy. To cure a nervous patient means to change his mental attitude, that is, to make him drop his romanticisms and intellectualisms and to substitute a realistic outlook. If this is accomplished, a mental attitude of self-trust is installed, and the physical and mental tools of the body can then aim straight at their goals, without fear, without self-consciousness, without morbid preoccupation.

EXCERPTS FROM DR. LOW'S ADDRESSES

1. *Self-Importance and Group-Importance*

"My husband wanted me to go to a movie with him," exclaimed the patient. "I felt hurt," she continued, "and thought can't he see how bad I feel?" Another patient reported that her feelings were hurt when her physician told her not to pay attention to her cough because it was "just nerves." "Wouldn't anybody's feelings be hurt," she went on, "if your own doctor brushed you off like that?" When patients complain in this manner about hurts to their feelings, what kind of feelings do they have in mind? I told you once (Recovery News, June 1950) about the difference between physical and mental feelings but will not dwell on this distinction today. You will recall, however, that I mentioned at the time that feelings are linked to beliefs. Your feeling of love for your mother is linked to the belief that she is a model of virtue, dependability and self-sacrifice; your feeling for your child is tied in with the belief that the boy is honest and trustworthy and well-mannered and that he will some day prove his mettle. The same holds true for your feelings toward your country. They are anchored in the belief that it has a glorious past, a fine constitution and an effective system of government. Should now anything happen that throws into question the dependability of your mother, the trustworthiness of your son, or the grandeur of your country, your beliefs will be shaken, and your feelings will be shocked. Note that the beliefs which I quoted bolster your sense of importance. They lend status to your quality as son, father, citizen. And since son and father are members of the family group, and since a citizen is part of the national group, you will understand that when I spoke of the sense of importance I meant the belief in, and feeling of, group-importance. You feel important as the son of this wonderful mother, or as the father of this splendid specimen of a son, or as the citizen of this incomparable nation. As such, your sense of group-importance is a value, as tender and vulnerable as values generally are. A hurt dealt a valuable belief is sheer rudeness, deplorable and perhaps inexcusable. But when my patients say their feelings are hurt, their complaints do not touch on the experience of group-importance but rather on such matters as a husband not noticing "how bad I feel," and a doctor classing a cough as "just nerves," or somebody not being invited to a party, or a birthday not being remembered, or a rushing busybody being kept waiting by the saleslady, the elevator man, the telephone operator or the grocer. In these instances, it is the trivial feeling of, and the paltry belief in, your *self-importance* which are hurt and shaken, not the noble feeling of, and lofty belief in, your group-importance. And if my patients insist on working themselves up over their "hurt feelings," I shall advise them that their complaints commonly refer to those inanities which spring from an inflated sense of self-importance, and that a hurt to one's self-importance is nothing more than a shock to one's personal vanity. I shall further advise them that they had better learn to spot their vanities, and that each time they are ready to mouth the empty phrase, "My feelings have been hurt," they should promptly recognize it as a vain belief in one's personal importance. The sense of group-importance commands respect, and the implied feelings and beliefs, being held in general esteem, will hardly ever be subject to hurts, that is, expressions of disrespect. But the sense of personal importance is nothing but an idle claim and silly pretense, and the best thing that can happen to it is to be hurt every once in a while. The occasional hurt will offer a welcome opportunity to practice spotting of vanities, shallowness and conceit.

2. The "Misunderstood" and "Unappreciated" Patient

A woman patient held forth with emphatic intensity, "I had lots of grief this week. My father-in-law died, and my son had a nasty cold. And the funeral in zero weather was no picnic either.... It just seems to me..." Another patient complained in a similar vein that all the sister does is to say the most discouraging things "all the time," and the mother does not understand her "at all," and the children irritate her "no end." Confronted with complaints of this kind I ask myself: What precisely do my patients expect of life. Do they expect eternal calm, unbroken serenity, an existence never so much as ruffled by irritation? Is it news to them that fathers-in-law die? that children have colds? that funerals may take place at zero or even subzero temperatures? And if children irritate parents or sisters make discouraging remarks or mothers fail to plumb the fathomless depth of a daughter's inner experiences, why don't my patients realize that all of this is part of life, nothing to get excited about, nothing to be shocked by, something, indeed, to be expected? The reason is, of course, that my patients are romanto-intellectualists, thinking of themselves as singular and of their experiences as exceptional. If they were realists they would know that in this imperfect world of ours very few people can escape "lots of grief this week" or any other week. And I have yet to see families in which sisters are always encouraging and mothers unfailingly understanding. The point I wish to make is that occurrences of the kind I mentioned are an unavoidable part of life which means: of average life. Unfortunately, a romanto-intellectualist refuses to think of himself as average. In his mind, life is not worth living unless it is intensely stirring, exciting and stimulating or *utterly* dangerous, *maximally* tragic, *incurably* bleak. You know that the latter is what I call the undesirable form of exceptionality.

Let us take a glance at the matter of not being understood. In the instance in which the mother was accused of not understanding the daughter, the latter delivered herself of a burst of self-pity which ran in the customary channels of mawkish sentimentality. "Honestly," she exploded, "that headache is more than I can stand. Why must I have all the bad luck in this world?" To which the mother replied calmly, "I have headaches, too, and they are not mild, either. But I refuse to raise a fuss over them."

What made the patient assume that this plain and unpretentious language revealed a lack of understanding? What was it that the mother misunderstood? She certainly had a good grasp of the nature of headaches. Her distinction between their mild and severe intensities represented good insight. Her logic was unimpeachable and her comprehension faultless when she intimated that pains can be borne patiently, as she did, or fussed about peevishly, as the daughter chose to do. The mortal sin which was charged against the mother was not that she misunderstood the daughter's utterance. It was rather that she did not agree with that daughter's opinion. She gave understanding but refused consent. And if an intellectualist is denied consent for his "smart" opinions, he feels—misunderstood. And if the "singular" feelings of a romanticist are not shared, his tender sentiments are—not properly appreciated. If this happens to my romanto-intellectualist patients they complain bitterly that their self-diagnosed emergencies are not taken seriously and that their hysterias and emotionalisms are not accepted at face value. Then, they cry out in despair that their thoughts are misunderstood and their feelings not appreciated. If this comes to pass, life seems to be deprived of its vital purpose, and the patient issues a pathetic wail that "fate is against me" and "everthing must happen to me" and "why can't I have luck once at least?" Then, existence which romanto-intellectualist fancy expects to be a perennial picnic turns into a never-ending panic, and simple events like those of a father-in-law dying or children having colds assume the dismal aspects of bleak calamities and tragic misfortunes. In Recovery, the patient is made to realize the fallacy of the romanticist estimate that life is either supreme bliss or dreary desolation. He learns that there is a middle ground of solid averageness in which the tonic quality of realistic action does away with the hectic hunt for picnics which have a sorry way of turning into panics.

EXCERPTS FROM DR. LOW'S ADDRESSES

1. *The Patient's "Confusions"—Chance or Purpose?*

"I've tried my level best," protested a woman patient, "but I cannot for the world of me stop working myself up. Can I help it if I'm confused and don't understand what you mean by spotting?" This is the stock excuse of sabotaging patients who claim a strange inability to understand when I ask them to spot and stop their self-diagnosing and their tempers. And the more thoroughly they "misunderstand" the more fiercely do they work themselves up, and all the while they insist that they "can't help it" although they try their "level best." As explanation they advance the claim that they are confused. But if confusion has any discernible meaning it means lack of discrimination, that is, an inability or difficulty to distinguish between one thing and another. It may also mean blunted judgment and obscured vision. What is it that the patient is unable to distinguish? Which are the happenings or observations that defy his judgment and elude his vision? I tell him to spot his symptoms as distressing but not dangerous. Does it require the mentality of a wizard to understand this clear statement? Or, I try to persuade him that symptoms are maintained by tenseness, and that to avoid tenseness he will have to control his temper. The average intellect can certainly grasp this simple formulation. Why, then, does the patient claim inability to understand? The fact is that the patient is told one thing by me and another by his symptoms. I tell him that his condition is a nervous ailment, severe but harmless. At the same time I assure him that I can and will cure him. As against this, his symptoms suggest an organic disease, threatening that he is doomed, that health will be denied him forever, that he cannot regain control of his functions. My message is one of optimism and encouragement, theirs one of pessimism and defeat. If a person is presented with two sets of contrary suggestions one would expect him to choose, nay, to grab the one which is more promising and more helpful. Why does the patient prefer to choose those suggestions which are menacing and harmful? Is confusion the proper explanation? I shall admit that if an individual is confused he will have difficulty choosing correctly. He will try and miss, will try again and perhaps miss again. But, assuredly, if he continues his trials he will be bound to make a hit sometimes. Confusion, it is true, makes for hit and miss scores. But even the most confused person will make a few hits among his many misses. However, when I listen to the complaints of my sabotaging patients they tend to have a perfect record of nothing but misses. How can a confusion yield a nearly perfect score, something like a one hundred percent result? A record of this kind cannot be achieved unless the person securing it has unerring discrimination, extreme determination and superb skill. Such a performance is impossible under conditions of confusion. And if my patients, asked to choose optimism instead of pessimism, somehow manage to obtain misses practically *all the time* and to score a hit practically *no time*, I shall advise them that a genuine confusion cannot possibly accomplish clear-cut results of this kind. This can only be the outcome of persistent planning and intending and wanting, that is, of design. True enough, the wanting and designing are not deliberate. They are intuitive. It is the intuitive desire to cling stubbornly and doggedly to the diagnosis of an organic condition and the equally intuitive tendency to retain temper. The inevitable conclusion is that the patient has excellent understanding of what I want him to do but prefers to plead a mythical confusion which permits him to continue his favorite game of sabotage. In all of this a principle is involved which I shall try to state as briefly as I can. You know, of course, that every act is either produced by chance or engineered by a purpose. The best known example of the operation of chance is a game of cards. Suppose a party of men play 100 games in succession. If everything is left to chance, it will be impossible for any one of the players to win all or nearly all of the 100 games. If he does we suspect fraud, that means, purpose. Chance operates on a fifty-fifty basis or close to it. Purpose, on the other hand, may produce a one hundred percent result or something close to it. If my patients play the game of manipulating symptoms on a one hundred percent basis or close to it, the inference is inescapable that a purpose is involved and not chance. The patient says he "can't help it" if he is in a state of confusion. The implication is that he is confused by chance which, of course, "cannot be helped." But if he is confused practically "all the time" the symptom is manipulated with nearly a one hundred percent regularity, which is unknown in the realm of chance but very well known in the domain of purpose.

A few more words about chance and purpose: Leaving your home after an argument with your wife you are in an ugly mood. A stranger approaches you asking for directions. Smarting yet from the effect of the preceding domestic quarrel, you return a discourteous answer. Presently a man turns up who is both a close friend and neighbor to you. Your mood brightens, and a pleasant conversation ensues. While you chat on, a merry flow of good-natured jokes and gay recollections, a person bumps into you, hurrying past without even the pretense of an apology. Your mood darkens again but instantly takes on a brighter hue when your genial neighbor, on taking leave, requests the honor of your visit to his new summer home. In this sequence of events, you had five separate experiences, three of them irritating (the temper spat with your wife, the inquiry of the stranger, the collision with the hurrying person); two were stimulating (the chat with the neighbor and the invitation to the summer cottage). All the encounters "happened by chance." None of them were produced by intent or purpose. The ratio of stimulation to irritation was two by three, close to the fifty-fifty ratio expected of chance happenings. Suppose now you are a salesman in a department store where customers foregather at your counter by sheer chance. Be certain that a great many of them will irritate you with senseless demands, unreasonable impositions or plain rudeness. Yet, your mood will remain even all the time. You will establish a 100 percent record of courtesy and will not permit your temper to "take chances" with the prospects of a sale. You do that because it is your set purpose to please all your clients regardless of the irritation they may "chance" to inflict on you. You will now understand that chance behavior "has no chance" when a purpose governs a situation.

You will also understand that if a patient has an almost *100 percent* record of "working himself up" or an almost *continuous* inability to understand what I tell him; if he complains *incessantly* and practically *never* succeeds in spotting his self-diagnosing; in other words, if he manages to "leave nothing to chance" in the matter of sabotaging the process of getting well; you will understand that such a well nigh 100 percent performance can be nothing but the outcome of a set purpose to obstruct the physician's effort. The difference between the salesman and that patient is that, with the one, the purpose of establishing a 100 percent record is deliberate and conscious while with the other it is intuitive and apart from consciousness. With the one, the purpose is group-minded, with the other it is self-minded. But whether conscious or intuitive, group-centered or self-centered, in either case, it is a determined will which acts "on purpose" and "leaves nothing to chance."

2. *"It Is Real; I Don't Imagine It."*

The patient's name, Bernice Olson, innocent though it was, proved fatal to her. The classmates discovered that the initials read B. O. After that they did not tire calling her, with smirks and sneers, "B.O.," sometimes even spelling it out "Body Odor." When I first examined her she was 16 years of age but looked back already on a life of loneliness, agony and frustration. She was treated successfully and recovered. While under treatment she insisted frequently that she really had that body odor, that she herself smelled it all the time, that she felt how it coursed through the body and rose in smelly waves from abdomen and back to chest and face. "It is a real odor," she protested eagerly and stubbornly, "it is not imagination."

After completing my examination, on the occasion of her first visit to my office, I assured her, of course, that the odor was nothing but a sensation, that I could not smell it and nobody else could. "I knew you would say that," she objected, "everybody tells me that. But I smell the odor, I can describe it, I feel how it moves inside. My clothes have the smell, and I have to change them several times a day. Nobody believes me, but the odor is real. I don't imagine it."

Bernice was not alone in this insistence that what she felt was not born of imagination but "honest-to-goodness" reality. She did what all my patients are likely to do. All or most of them are prone to insist that they are right and I am wrong, that their opinion is correct and mine incorrect. The one patient complains that people stare at him and hastens to add that they "really" stare, that it is not imagination. Another patient is ready to swear by all that is holy that he "really" does not sleep, or that something "really" presses in his brain; that the air-hunger is "really" choking the life-breath out of him, or that the fatigue has "really" exhausted his muscles. When patients contend so ardently and passionately that what they experience is "real," what they wish to imply is that they tell the truth. To them it is an unshakable principle that when a thing looks or feels real it is an objective fact, true, actually existing, undeniable.

Not so long ago a patient told me that his head shakes. "You have just to look at my head and you see the tremor. I can see it by the way the rim of my hat shakes." I looked at him and had him put on his hat but could see no tremor, with or without the hat on. I then asked him to look in the mirror, placed a large sheet of white paper on his head and demonstrated to him that the sheet showed no evidence of shaking or any kind of motion. He admitted that if the head shook the tremor would be bound to transmit itself to the paper but was far from convinced. "That's all right, doctor," he said, "nevertheless I feel the shaking. It is real, I don't imagine it." I explained to him: "You think that if a thing is felt as real it is true. But there is nothing that looks more real than the hallucination of an alcoholic person who "sees" a snake coiling ready to strike him. And there is no doubt in the mind of a delusional patient that the man who just stepped out of the wall, pointing a gun at him, is real and not imagined. And to quote an example out of the experience of mentally well people: Is there any thing in this world that could possibly look more real than the tiger who jumps at you in your dream? That tiger is seen—in the wild fantasy of your dream—with a most extraordinary vividness. You feel his hot breath, you see the fire in his eyes, the ferocious expression in his face. The experience is so horribly "real" that you can describe the most minute texture of each single part of his body, and yet, would you maintain that the tiger which you see in your dream is "real?"

It is time that my patients should realize that the more "real" a sight looks, or a feeling feels the weaker is its claim to being rated as "really" seen or "really" felt. And my advice to you is that once a sensation or impulse or feeling impresses you as "so utterly real" you may be certain it is imagined and not at all real. And if anyone of you will ever again dare defend and fight for the reality of what you notice inside you, I shall simply tell you that hallucinations, delusions and dreams have the highest degree of reality, and that if a thing looks real it is almost certain to be nothing but imagined.

EXCERPTS FROM DR. LOW'S ADDRESSES

1. *The Patient's Disabilities, Will or Fate?*

The patient, a man of mature age, had been suffering from a depression for two years when I first saw him. His symptoms were of the ordinary description: difficulty of sleeping, mechanical appetite, reduced interests and lowered feelings. His spontaneity was gravely affected, hence, even simple tasks required the utmost in effort. Previously, a person brimming with energy and confidence, he was now left without ambition and initiative, fearful of making up his mind, unable to plan and decide. Adding to the misfortune was the fact that in his protracted career of idleness, he developed ugly and disturbing habits. He paced the floor in rapid strides and abrupt turns practically all day and a good part of the night, all the while emitting peculiar yells, a strange mixture of sobbing, moaning, barking and screaming. "He acts like a caged animal," was the way his wife described his behavior. Finally, the neighbors complained to the landlord, and the couple were in danger of being evicted.

I asked the patient, "Why do you yell so that the neighbors become aroused? And why do you keep pacing the floor until you are exhausted?" His reply was, "I have to do it. If I stop I get so tense that I fear I'll burst." I remarked, "I have observed you in classes and noticed that you are able to sit through addresses and interviews for an hour and longer without rising from your seat and without voicing even a feeble sound. I also know that you control your behavior to perfection while sitting in my reception room, waiting for your turn of treatment. I watched you on several of these occasions and witnessed an almost spectacular tenseness on your face. Nevertheless, you made no move to dash out of the room, nor did you yell or bark. My conclusion is that you are well able, even with an extreme tenseness working toward the "bursting" point, to hold down the impulse to race or scream when you are in Recovery or in my office. If you can check your reactions in some places, why do you *have to* release them in others?" "Well," said the patient, "I don't understand it myself. But it is true that I can control on the outside, and at home *I can't.*"

What I want you to note here are the phrases *"I have to"* and *"I can't."* All the complaints of my patients can be reduced to and properly fitted into the pattern of these two phrases. All of them complain that they have to do things which they do not want to do at all, and that they cannot do other things which they want to do badly. There is the patient with the "intolerable" nervous cough. At home he embarks on an unrestrained campaign of furious coughing and rasping, claiming the tickle in the throat is "unbearable." But when he is among people, his versatile tracheal and bronchial tissues somehow manage to exhibit a perfect set of "company manners," behaving as well-bred throats always do, neither coughing nor rasping. A similar situation obtains in the case of the patient who, troubled with an "intractable" itch, scratches ferociously at home but conveniently suspends both the itching and the scratching on the street, in buses, at parties and theatres. Outside the home these patients have no difficulty controlling and stopping the same ugly habit which they *have to* indulge and *can't* stop once they step inside the home. How is it possible that a person can use his Will at 10 PM at the theatre but is utterly deprived of even a trace of that same Will at 11 PM at home? There are legitimate occasions when an individual has to do things opposed by his Will and can't do other things approved by it. Situations of this kind are produced by organic diseases. A man who has sustained a fracture of the leg has the Will to go to work but "can't" and has no Will to lie in bed but "has to." The same rule applies to cancers, pneumonias, infections, and all manner of organic ailments. Patients afflicted with any of these organic disorders cannot perform as they would and have to perform as they would not. In conditions of this nature the disease ordained by *Fate* stymies the *Will* possessed by the personality. But have you ever heard of a cancer which is always present at home and regularly disappears at special times in special localities? Or of a fracture in which the bones dangle wildly whenever the patient is among the members of his family but are invariably well set and conducting themselves properly at social functions? How can cancered organs and fractured extremities distinguish between the social meaning of the home where they can act as they please (exercising sovereignty) and outside engagements where they have to submit to rules and standards (practicing fellowship)? You will agree that this would be the height of absurdity. Organic diseases do not, of course, change their behavior in accord with the social meaning of the situation. Such *selective and discriminating* behavior is impossible under conditions in which Fate reigns. Organic disturbances, that is, complications created by Fate, act indiscriminately and without selection. They may strike any person at any time in any place. Once they have struck they do not pick out shrewdly certain occasions in which they will make a stage appearance or certain others in which they will keep cunningly off the stage. If a symptom is regularly present in one set of conditions and regularly absent in another, the judicious choice cannot be the result of Fate which is never selective. It must be the outflow of Will whose very function is to choose and select.

In stating that "choosy" and selective symptoms point to a Will making the choice and determining the selection, I do not mean to imply that the patient wants to create or retain his disturbance. Nothing is further from my mind than an insinuation of this kind. My patients want to get well, of course. And if they are ill, the illness is certainly not of their choosing. It would be preposterous to hold them responsible for their condition. That condition is produced by Fate, not by Will. It is Fate, and nothing else, which saddles a person with choking sensations and fatigues and depressions. And whether it is possible to prevent the development and onset of nervous conditions I simply do not know. I have seen multitudes of persons who were as well as anybody might wish to be efficient, gay, generous, well-adjusted personally and socially, and yet they contracted a nervous ailment. Many of them were struck by their nervous trouble "out of a blue sky," without warning, without any preceding disturbance. They were suddenly seized with a spell of air-hunger while they were waiting for the next street car to pass by. Or, they attended a show in the pink of health, and while they were enjoying the performance, fully absorbed and not a bit tense or self-conscious, an arm went limp, or an ear went deaf, or an "explosion" rocked the brain. Nothing in the present or previous behavior of the victims could possibly explain the abrupt occurrences which were utterly unexpected. A great number of my patients experienced their first symptoms during a pleasure-packed party or on the occasion of a stimulating card game, at innocent family gatherings or on a carefree walk, or under similar circumstances which were singularly free from irritation. The affliction came out of nowhere. It simply "happened" and was undoubtedly not created by any intention on the part of the stricken person. It was Fate and not Will which initiated the disorder and the attendant panic. But once the patient was examined and given instructions how to get well, once a program was mapped out for him for the purpose of piloting his nervous system back to adjustment, did he honestly accept the plan and sincerely carry out the instructions? The answer is clear: Some of my patients cooperate and some sabotage. And whether you are given to thorough cooperation or indulge in reckless sabotage does not depend on Fate but entirely on your Will. My patients are not responsible for the type of their ailment or the mode of its onset. But emphatically, they are responsible for the type and degree of their cooperation. And what I here call Will is primarily the determination to cooperate wholly and faithfully. If I instruct a patient to use his muscles, to give up self-diagnosing and to control his temper and he counters with the silly excuses of "I can't" or "I have to," these dodges and hedges are decidedly the products of his Will and by no means unintentional accidents produced by Fate.

You will now understand that such phrases as "I have to," "I can't," or "I try my best but can I help it if I don't succeed?" mean that the patient diagnoses his condition as a physical disease in which Fate has paralyzed his Will. No matter how skillfully fitting is the context in which phrases of this kind are used, they mean nothing less than the diagnosis of an organic ailment. They mean that the patient refuses to accept the physician's diagnosis of a distressing but harmless nervous disturbance insisting on self-diagnosing it as a serious organic ailment. The tragedy is that self-diagnosing is anything but an innocent pastime. It breeds defeatism and fatalism, continued tenseness and endless agony. If the nervous patient is to escape the tragedy of self-diagnosing, he will have to employ our spotting techniques with particular force whenever he thinks or voices the defeatist and fatalistic phrases "I have to," "I can't," or "Can I help it if...?"

DR. LOW'S COLUMN
TO SPOT IS TO KNOW THAT YOU DON'T KNOW

"I feel that pressure over the chest," said the patient with obvious irritation, "and *naturally* I think of my heart." He then continued in a similar vein: "A friend of mine recently collapsed on the street and died from a heart attack. He had been under a doctor's care, and the electrocardiogram was negative. Do you blame me if I can't forget that?"

This patient had the sensation of chest pressure. This was an *experience*. Noticing the pressure he thought his heart was bad. This was a *belief*. Some time later, he had another experience, that of a friend dying on the street from a heart attack. He then thought (believed) that this accident was extraordinary that nobody could blame him if he couldn't "forget that." And all of it he considered (believed) perfectly "natural." But knowing the patient to be a victim of palpitations and being haunted by the fear of death I deem (believe) it perfectly "natural" to conclude that when Karl—so we shall call the man—heard of his friend's sudden death, the thought (belief) leaped into his brain that he was next in line for a similar fate. And my final conclusion is that the bulk of the suffering which is the lot of my patients does not stem from their "dreadful" experiences but rather from their frightening beliefs. And today I propose to speak to you about the disastrous effect which your beliefs have on your inner experiences.

If you say that you believe something you mean to imply that you Know little or nothing about it. A belief is an opinion, an assumption, a theory, but emphatically not knowledge. Knowledge means certainty or near-certainty, belief means unsureness. Seeing this piece of furniture before which I am seated you know it is a table; you do not merely believe it. Similarly, when you experience a spasm in your chest you know that something is pressing there. But if you say it is the heart which does the cramping and the pressing, this you merely believe and do not know for sure. Experiences are facts which convey knowledge, beliefs are imaginations which connote lack of knowledge. The statement, "I believe" means "I imagine" or "I lack knowledge" or "I know that I do not know." An imagination (belief) is a guess and may at times be a correct guess. If you go on guessing day after day, hour after hour, the chances are you will sometimes guess right (by sheer chance). But if guessing is practiced continuously in the vital field of health the practice turns into a habit which is pernicious because it prevents you from acquiring certain knowledge. And without certainty life becomes an endless chain of doubt, of fear of the unknown and anxiety about what may strike next.

To frame and hold beliefs is a thoroughly legitimate activity of the mind. You cannot act unless you first form an opinion, reflectively or intuitively, whether the planned action is correct, wise, safe. The opinion which you adopt is based either on certain knowledge or on guessing belief. A man advances toward you from a distance, and you believe it is your friend Joe. As he comes nearer you realize that your belief was erroneous and *decide* it is George and not Joe. The belief which you held about Joe is now dropped. Mark here that beliefs can be held or dropped. You drop a belief if you decide it is incorrect. Which means that whether you hold on to a belief or drop it depends on your decision. And your decisions are the acts of your Will. The Will accepts or rejects beliefs; it agrees or disagrees with them; it prefers one kind of belief to another; it discards this one and retains that one. Some beliefs are declared by the Will to be valuable, others valueless, some harmless and some dangerous. We conclude that beliefs and disbeliefs are decisions made by the Will. We further conclude that with regard to beliefs, there are two kinds of Wills: THE WILL TO BELIEVE and THE WILL TO DISBELIEVE.

When Karl felt a pressure in the chest his mind made ready to form an opinion (belief) of what the experience meant. It might have been one of those pressures which he had felt on numerous occasions in numerous places, in head, chest, abdomen, arms and legs. They were of a transient nature, came and went, returned and left again. Sometimes they pressed lightly, at other times more intensely. The very fact that they were regularly given to erratic and ephemeral behavior marked them as innocent disturbances. If Karl's chest sensation was one of these trivial and transient pressures he could have decided or formed the belief that what he felt in the chest was harmless and not worth his attention. He might also have remembered my dictum that chest pressure is in most instances due to spasms of the muscles above or between the ribs and that they are produced by strain, excitement

63

and preoccupation. These and other possibilities of explaining the sensation were known to Karl. He could have chosen any of them. But he decided to choose the dismal theory of a dangerous heart ailment. What prompted him to make this disastrous decision?

When Karl "decided," that is, formed and accepted the belief that the pressure over his chest meant a heart ailment he made a diagnosis. You will agree that a diagnosis presupposes thorough knowledge about the nature of diseases. It cannot be made on the basis of flimsy guesses or clumsy beliefs. Knowledge, I told you, means certainty. Did Karl assume that he possessed the necessary certain knowledge required of a competent diagnostician? Preposterous as it may seem to impute to a patient a silly arrogance of this kind, nevertheless, this arrogant attitude must be charged to Karl and to everyone of my patients. They all arrogate to themselves the privilege of self-diagnosing and are fully aware that in doing so they commit an act of gross sabotage. That they are aware of sabotaging is evident from the manner in which they "give themselves away." Karl gave himself away naively and unthinkingly when he said that he "naturally" had to think of a heart ailment. The "naturally" meant: What else could I have thought of but a heart condition? That was the natural thing to consider! You see, in nature, a river is a river, a bird a bird, and a stone a stone. "Naturally, they can't be anything else! In matters human, things are not that simple, not that "natural." The pain experienced by a human being is not just a pain. It is also upsetting or patiently borne, curable or incurable, treated or neglected, abating or progressing. The pain viewed with despair is totally different from the one faced with fortitude. Some pains are "just nervous" and nothing to worry about, others organic and due to a serious ailment. You see here that, in human beings, one and the same thing may appear in many shapes, perhaps in uncounted variations. In nature, this does not happen. These things are or are supposed to be forever the same, unchanging, stable, permanent, immutable. There are many ways of thinking about and explaining things human. But there are "no two ways of thinking" about nature. Things have there a one-way meaning only. And you express this incontrovertible, certain and one-way meaning of natural processes by saying, "naturally I had to..." or "naturally it is so. How could it be otherwise?" When Karl said, "...and naturally I think of my heart..." he gave away the secret that, voicing a questionable belief, he tried to wrap it in the deceptive phrasing of a knowledge so certain that it seemed a "natural" fact and the only possible diagnosis of the condition.

This is the crux of the matter: My patients have the imperative desire to make their own diagnoses. You will fully understand the force and urgency of this desire if you will reflect for a moment what a diagnosis means. You will then realize that everybody makes diagnoses every minute of his life. You see a package neatly wrapped on your desk. Instantly you want to make sure what it contains. You examine its contents and find it is a birthday gift for you. These are the "findings" in the "case" disclosed by your "examination." They yield the "diagnosis" of the birthday gift. Or, you come across a book with an appealing title or read a sensational headline in the newspaper and wish to ascertain what the book and the headline contain. You examine them and, again, find or diagnose their contents. You see, in life everything has an outer appearance or surface and an inner substance or contents. And the human mind is forever eager and curious to penetrate through the surface down to the contents of things. The contents are inside, and in order to know what precisely is "within" you must examine to "find out." In doing this you make a diagnosis. The human body is notorious for having the most tantalizing and most mysterious contents, some of them agonizing and frightening, some comforting and soothing, but all of them arousing curiosity and stimulating interest. Being hidden away "within," their meaning cannot be "found out" except through proper examination. Unfortunately there is no ready method available to the untrained person for opening and unwrapping the interior of the body and for examining its contents. The art of diagnosing the inner secrets of the body is reserved for those who are specially trained to practice it, that is, for expert diagnosticians who must be physicians, of course. If the patient, driven on by his diagnostic furor, insists on finding out what the processes wrapped up within his body mean, he will be impelled by his ever-restless curiosity to formulate a "diagnosis" of his own. But this so-called diagnosis, being a jumble of crude guesses, will gain him nothing but wild confusion, rambling assumptions and shaky conclusions. If what he sets out to diagnose are symptoms the chances are he will guess that his palpitations mean the threat of collapse, his chest pains the danger of heart disease and the death of a friend the ominous warning that he will be next. The results will be fear and suffering, horror and agony. If the patient is to escape his self-induced horrors and agonies he will have to spot, continuously and untiringly, his unholy bent for self-diagnosing and will have to know, the very moment he experiences a symptom, that all he can do is to guess its meaning but to know little or nothing about it. Then he will have to remember immediately, through trigger-spotting, that guessing is the reverse of knowing. If he does that honestly and conscientiously he will get to know that he does not know. And if you wish to gain expertness in the art of spotting all you will have to do is to have your mind constantly on the truth that to spot correctly is to know that you do not know. Unless you keep this truth persistently in your consciousness you will be an unhappy and helpless victim of your Will to Believe (your own diagnostic guesses). Spotting, that is, the ever-awake knowledge in diagnosing will make you adopt the Will to Disbelieve (your own diagnostic guesses). It will make you accept the physician's certain knowledge and will do away with sabotage and its attendant horrors and agonies, its panics and vicious cycles. And after hearing this exposition about knowing which is certainty and about guessing which is ignorance you will no longer, I hope, assail my ears with such blatant statements as: "Honestly, doctor, I have tried the hardest to spot but I simply don't know how to do it." My answer will be: If you have the modesty and humility to know that you don't know your spotting will be of the most perfect and exquisite quality. If you have difficulty in the practice of spotting the evidence is that you lack the modesty and humility to know that you do not know.

THE PHILOSOPHY OF RECOVERY, INC.*
ORDER, BELIEFS, CONVICTIONS

Philosophies are of two kinds. The one presumes to tell you what the world is and means, how it came into being and what will be its fate. This is what is called a *philosophy of the world.* One of these philosophies claims that in this world of ours everything is matter, another that all is mind. The one insists that the world was created, the other that it evolved. There are philosophies of optimism which conceive of the universe as moving toward progressive development, and others which preach a bleak pessimism according to which chance and fate alone govern our destiny with the road leading ultimately and unavoidably to a final annihilation of life and disintegration of matter. We in Recovery have nothing to do with philosophical constructions of this sort. They may be true or false, noble or vulgar, inspiring or depressing, but to us they are irrelevant because they do not touch on the principle of our vital issue which is concerned with daily life and not with universal existence or eternal being. If we are to formulate a philosophy it will have to be a *philosophy of life,* more particularly one of daily life, emphatically not a philosophy of the world. If in the following remarks I shall use the word philosophy you will know that what I refer to is not what makes the world go around but rather what keeps the functions of this our body and of this our daily life in healthy order or throws them into ailing disorder.

When a patient comes to consult me his complaint is in essence that some of his functions are out of order. He remembers that prior to his present nervous ailment his heart used to beat "in perfect order," while now it sets up wild palpitations; that his previously "orderly" breathing is now frequently "disordered" by recurring spells of air-hunger; that his thought processes which were wont to proceed in well-ordered progression are now deranged (disordered) by "brain storms," "racing thoughts," obsessions and compulsions. In all these instances, the patient holds the view that his nervous and mental functions, that is, his thoughts, feelings, sensations and impulses ought to be governed by a set pattern of concrete order. A theory of this kind is a philosophy. It carries the philosophical belief that life is or ought to be ordered by a stable, relatively unchanging principle. That

*Paper read at the First National Convention of Recovery, Inc. November 4, 1951.

principle, the patient thinks, calls for such elements as balance, equilibrium, perhaps for the golden rule and the solid middle road. All of these he reflects, constitute order which is health. If they are absent or disturbed, it means disorder which is disease. There can be hardly any disagreement concerning this part of the patient's philosophy. It is compounded of common sense and common experience, hence, can become part and parcel of the philosophy of Recovery.

Order is either stable or unstable. The manner in which the individual particles of a stone are arranged (ordered) is always the same. Kick the stone with violence, hurl it with force against another stone, expose it to rain, fire, hurricane, it will nevertheless retain its "natural order," its character and stability. If you lop off one half its bulk or grind it into innumerable bits of matter, each part will be smaller in size but will still have the character of a stone. We say: a stone has a stable order. The simplest example which I can offer of unstable order occurring in nature is a river. In winter its surface freezes; in spring it swells beyond its ordinary level; in summer it loses moisture and shrinks. Sometimes it is muddy, at other times it is crystal-clear. But no matter how spectacular and dramatic may be its changes, its fundamental character is forever the same. It is always and unchangeably a body of water, frozen water, running water, muddied water, limpid water. We say: in the realm of *material nature* the order of things is not basically influenced by changes in weather, season and other environmental factors. Stable or unstable, things in nature invariably maintain their order. This is different in the case of *human nature*. A mature human being, let me say, an adult man, lives on many levels. In the family he is father, husband, son, brother. In the community he is neighbor, friend, employer, employee, member of a club, citizen, teacher, adviser, leader, follower. Consider his function as a husband. Having been an "orderly" husband for years, loving his wife, adoring the chidren, working for them, sharing their joys and sorrows, he is suddenly seized with an ugly suspicion that his wife is not loyal. Previously, the pattern on which his marital life was ordered was that of implicit trust. Now the pattern has changed into an abiding distrust, bitterness and craving for revenge. In past days, he never thought of questioning the wife's character, of doubting her morals, of spying on her activities and movements, or of torturing her with revolting insinuations. Now he does nothing else. Formerly he was a loving marriage partner, now he is a hating partisan. His home life, once the source of untold delights, of peace and happiness, is now a place of turmoil, strife, gloom and cheerlessness. Everything within and around him has undergone a radical change. In days bygone he used to turn his interest and attention to a multitude of topics and endeavors, delighting in joint family action, in picnics, shows, sports and trips. He took part in civic affairs, visited freely back and forth, pottered gayly around the house. But now his mind is invariably and exclusively focused on his wild obsessions and fierce suspicions. You see here how in a human being the entire order of thinking, feeling and acting can be transformed, by a mere suspicion, into its exact opposite, from love to hatred, from selflessness to selfishness, from peacefulness to hostility, from trust to distrust. We say: in an adult human being, the order in which life is adjusted is so unstable that one single element—in our example, suspicion—can lastingly upset it so that it turns into its exact opposite.

A suspicion is a belief. If I say, "I believe," I wish to indicate that "I do not know," that, instead, "I merely believe." On the other hand, if I say, "This is a lamp," I mean to imply that I know for certain what the object is. I do not merely believe that "this is a lamp" but have certain knowledge that it is one. Should I say, "I believe this is a lamp"; I would suggest that my statement represents a belief instead of knowledge, moreover, that I am aware of not knowing for sure whether the object in question is a lamp. Which means that by using the phrase, "I believe," I intend to state that I am aware of the fact that I do not know for certain what kind of an object or person I deal with. To put it differently: The moment I use the word "belief" or "believing" or any of its synonyms, I want it to be understood that I voice a tentative opinion, that my assumption may be incorrect, and that should I discover its incorrectness I am ready to drop and change the belief. Strange as it may sound, the philosophy of Recovery is based unqualifiedly and unreservedly on this matter of belief. All its techniques have for their aim the intention to plant in the patient's mind the correct beliefs (about nervous health) offered by the physician and to purge it of the false beliefs held by himself. The reason for our almost fanatical preoccupation with the subject of beliefs is that it is they which either order or disorder the lives of mature human beings. With us in Recovery it is an axiom that while a nervous ailment is not necessarily caused by distorted beliefs, nevertheless, if it persists beyond a reasonable time, its continuance, stubbornness and "resistance" are produced by continuing, stubborn and "resisting" beliefs. The above quoted case of the jealous husband whose whole life was "thrown out of order" by a disrupting belief (jealousy) ought to be sufficiently convincing. But jealousy, it may be objected, is not exactly a nervous ailment, and whether or not beliefs have actually a decisive impact on the course of psychoneurotic conditions ought to be demonstrated by the quotation of the case history of a "real" psychoneurotic patient. Here, then, is the case of Harold: One day he was sitting at his desk, thinking of nothing in particular, relaxed to the point of being serene. Suddenly, "out of a blue sky," he was stricken with a wave of fear. What precisely he feared he did not know. He merely knew that fear was "coursing through the body." He felt faint and numb, had the impulse to yell and rush for help but controlled himself. Soon the fear left while a subtle apprehension remained. In the morning, the scare was gone but the apprehension still persisted, although its intensity lessened. After a few days Harold was "his former self again," except that an occasional fatigue or some fleeting pain and ache tended to remind him for a minute or so of the frightening incident. All went well until, one evening, he came across an article in the daily health column in which a medical journalist told his unsuspecting readers that heart diseases may begin with fatigue, pain over the chest and a fast heart-beat on exertion. Harold instantly felt a sharp pain over the left chest. He remembered the fatigue which he had recently experienced, recalled that "frightful" spell of some weeks ago and was convinced he had a heart ailment and was doomed to lead the life of a cripple or was threatened with collapse.

Harold's case is instructive. Before the wave of fear struck him he was tolerably relaxed. Being relaxed he felt (believed he was) secure. The suddenly rising fear and the subsequent apprehension changed the belief of security into that of insecurity. He recovered, however, spontaneously which means that he dropped his belief of insecurity and returned to his original belief of security. But when after reading the health column which, striking unnecessary terror into the hearts of innocent readers, ought to be called more properly the health calumny, his feeling (belief) of insecurity returned with elemental strength. This strength it gathered from the fact that the belief was now fortified by the authority of a medical editor. The loose belief had now become a solid conviction.

This example aptly portrays the condition in which all our patients find themselves. Up to a certain turn in their lives they are able to relax with reasonable success. Then the belief grips them, on the occasion of some harmless but frightening spell, that they are in danger and in need of help. That belief may not gain the strength of a firm conviction until some suggestion is offered by some questionable "authority," usually a radio announcer or journalist, that their condition may be the beginning of a dreadful disease. The "authority" which sometimes may be nothing more authentic than the story told by a neighbor of "a similar case" which ended fatally, clinches the *weak belief* into a *firm conviction*. In time, the conviction becomes more convincing. It gathers unto itself the strength of a dogma and resists every attempt to drop or change it. The longer the conviction lasts the more thoroughly does it disorder the life of the patient. It creates sustained tenseness, panics and vicious cycles, finally, the well known chain of nervous symptoms. On seeing the patient at that stage, the physician endeavors to divest him of the conviction of insecurity. But whether he will be successful depends on whether the patient will or will not accept (be convinced of) the physician's assurances. If the patient balks, engaging in the familiar game of self-diagnosing, a fight ensues between the convictions of the physician and those of the patient. This is called "resistance" or "sabotage." What the patient resists and sabotages is the physician's knowledge that nervous ailments require Will-training, Self-discipline and Self-control. What he fights for is his own conviction that he needs outside help for an ailment which has nothing to do with Will, discipline or control. The clash of the two antagonists is backed by two philosophies, mutually exclusive, contradictory and irreconcilable. The one is the philosophy of Self-control, the other that of Self-indulgence. If the philosophy of the physician prevails the result will be health, that is, restoration of order. If that of the patient wins, the ultimate outcome will be chronicity, that is, enduring disorder.

The distinction between loose beliefs and firm convictions is basic to an understanding of the Recovery philosophy. If my patients had nothing but beliefs with regard to their tempers and symptoms my therapeutic task would be easy. I would tell them that their beliefs are incorrect; that they are based on "nothing more convincing" than faulty conceptions, untenable premises and deficient experience. As against this, I would remind them that my conceptions, premises and experience have the merit of long years of study, research and training. This bit of instruction alone, if willingly accepted, might be sufficient to effect a change of attitude. Professional expertness would be pitted against lay ignorance, and the fair minded sufferer might be ready to exchange good-naturedly his own naive guess for the authoritative knowledge of the expert. The process might require a measure of discussion and explanation, and—in Recovery—the demonstration in classes that other patients regained their health after they changed their beliefs. Unfortunately, the finest demonstration, the most skillful discussion and most lucid explanation are no match for a solidly entrenched conviction. A person who holds a settled conviction is committed to it; he is ready, and perhaps eager, to defend it, to fight for it, to uphold it against evidence. With a person of this kind there is no discussion, no healthy exchange of views, no realistic testing of opinions. What he is itching for is to battle for his own conviction and to "knock out" the conviction of the partner. This person, be he a nervous patient or some other representative of the romanto-intellectualist breed, has no relish for getting things explained or discussed. What he wants is a fiery debate, not a calm discussion. Otherwise, how could you understand the paradox that my patients, supposedly seeking help and advice, resent and reject the advice which I offer. The answer is that, though suffering acutely, my patients are for some reason vitally interested in maintaining and upholding what they conceive of as their convictions. The one, being depressed, is convinced that all hope is lost, and if I assure him that his conviction is wrong he makes an heroic effort to convince me that I am wrong. The other has palpitations and along with it the conviction that his heart is damaged, and when I offer him my authoritative knowledge that his heart is in good order he clings to his conviction that his diagnosis is correct and mine incorrect. It is all weird, unsound and absurd, but that is precisely what naive, untested and haphazard convictions are likely to be: weird, unsound and absurd.

72

DR. LOW'S COLUMN
THE PRACTICE OF "STEPPING IN AND TAKING OVER"

Mathilde's husband, Fred, was examined and told that his blood pressure was elevated, though by no means excessively. "The pressure is fairly high," the physician said, "but there is nothing to worry about." In spite of this assurance the wife became alarmed to the point of developing panics when the husband merely sneezed. She realized that the fear was absurdly exaggerated but could not throw it off. "I try the hardest," she said, "to get the thought out of my mind but I simply can't." And another patient was obsessed with the idea that her brain was damaged. Although she knew, from persistent Recovery training, that this was sabotage in the form of self-diagnosing she pleaded inability to forget. And patients without number have assured me that they "try and try" to get rid of a disturbing idea but "it just doesn't work." My standard reply to remarks of this kind is that if I try to shake off an upsetting or ugly thought I invariably fail, no matter how hard I may "try and try" until I recognize that I don't know how to do it and give up the futile effort.

To forget means to let a memory die away, to permit it to drop out of consciousness. How a memory dies or fades away nobody knows. But the brain knows very well how to do the job of forgetting because it does it continuously. The brain knows how to forget and how to remember; it knows how to release impulses and how to restrain them. It registers sensations with exactitude and expertness and stores images in faithful reproduction of reality; it maintains the stream of thought in exquisite order and responds to stimulation and irritation with astonishing accuracy. All of this it does without special training and without any need for supervision. All organs of a healthy body perform their work on this pattern of skill and technical dexterity. They know what to do and how to do it. The heart knows how to supply exactly the amount of blood to the organs as and when they need it; the lungs know how to increase and decrease their rate of breathing as the situation requires, and the stomach and intestines are unquestioned masters in the performance of the functions of digestion and absorption. And assuredly, the eyes know how to see, the legs how to walk, the arms how to touch, grasp and lift. No doubt, our organs are perfectly capable of taking care of the functions assigned to them. What is more important is the fact that while they know how to do their work, we, their proud possessors, do not know how they do it. They are our knowing tools and we their ignorant owners. If left to themselves, they function smoothly and promptly. If we, the ignorant masters, decide and dare to interfere with their activities we are certain to throw them into disorder. That's what my patients do. For some reason they suspect their organs of being faulty. Then they watch and spy on their functions, try "the hardest" to direct and redirect them. But being utterly ignorant and inexperienced their only effect is to dislodge, disorder and dislocate the originally well ordered and well arranged performance. Mathilde gave a telling illustration of the process. Distrustful of her memory, she viewed it with suspicion, watched and spied on it, finally disturbing it so effectively that she could no longer get it going even when she "tried the hardest."

What precisely did Mathilde do when she tried to initiate the act of forgetting? The answer is that she did the reverse of what she ought to have done. I told you that forgetting means to let an experience drop out of consciousness, that is, to let it sink into oblivion. But when Mathilde labored to forget her husband's blood pressure she kept her mind continuously on the topic of blood pressure. Perhaps the thought "tried" to sink into oblivion. But how could it if Mathilde's overwrought mind, constantly preoccupied with the disturbing thought, refused to let it escape the sphere of awareness? Preoccupied with the issue of blood pressure, her whole thinking, all her reflective powers, her entire attention were forcibly focused on the subject. How could she ever hope to forget the item if she insisted on retaining it in her memory all the time? If her mind dealt incessantly with the physician's pronouncement, how could she expect to drop it out of the same mind with which she constantly thought about it? "Oh," she sobbed and agonized, "if I only could forget what the doctor said to Fred! Why did he have to tell him about the blood pressure? Now I shall always have to think of Fred and the danger that threatens him. Isn't it awful that I can't forget that thought?" In her merciless effort to forget she worked herself up to a frenzy which left room for no other thought but the one she ached to forget. In trying "the hardest" to forget she did everything to remember "the longest."

Mathilde's behavior points up the common tendency of my patients to step in and take over the functions of their organs whenever they notice or merely imagine a disturbed performance. In order to understand the supreme folly of such a procedure you must picture to yourself what would happen to a factory if the owner should decide to "step in and take over" the function of, let me say, the boiler attendant. Perhaps the owner was annoyed by what he considered excessive belching of smoke from the chimney. Now, in a fit of anger, he intercedes and does his own stoking. But being inexperienced he naturally produces far more smoke than the attendant ever did. Or, he was displeased with the work of the bookkeeper and, "stepping in and taking over," messed up the accounting department.

When the owner of the factory, in a fit of anger, "stepped in and took over," he acted from temper. He considered his employees wrong and incapable and himself right and competent. It was his temper which upset the orderly operation of the factory and turned order into disorder. This is exactly what my patients do when they "step in and take over" the supposedly deranged functions of their organs. Their department (organ) of memory annoys them, their palpitating heart displeases them, or their air-hungry lungs make them apprehensive, and they are seized either with fear or anger. Then, "stepping in and taking over," they disturb the previously ordered functions.

What my patients will have to learn is that if I accept them for treatment I do so because, after due examination, I decided that theirs is a nervous condition and that their organs are "in perfect order" and thoroughly capable of taking care of themselves. Your organs know how to restore order, but you don't know. If they are to do their job of keeping order they must not be interfered with. If they are watched and spied on and subjected to a senseless flood of silly orders from you, their incompetent owner, they become deranged, and your temper and your nervousness communicate themselves to them. Then they fail of their customary craftsmanship, and bungle their performance. Your organs are your competent and faithful servants. If they are left to themselves they perform with skill and precision. If you "step in and take over," they become deranged and produce symptoms.

The practice of "stepping in and taking over" is not by any

means an exclusive characteristic of my patients. It is a common habit found among numerous people in all states of health and in all walks of life. Mothers are particularly guilty of this failing. They have a special talent for irritating and exasperating their offspring by offering to do things for them which they would prefer to do themselves. Mothers of this kind are called possessive, and their stock phrases are, "let me do it for you," or, "let me show you, honey." With this, they stifle the initiative of their growing children and weaken or kill their spontaneity. Wives tend to be in the same category. Many of them, especially if they have no children, exhibit an annoying possessiveness toward their mates. They meddle with the private and business affairs of their husbands, question them endlessly whether they "really feel good today," insist that the husband is tired and in need of rest, remind him each morning not to forget gloves, rubbers or handkerchief, and not infrequently force him to swallow homebrewed or advertised medication because they are sure "father doesn't feel well." Mathilde had always been a possessive wife of this description. She was addicted to a well nigh irresistible urge to "manage" Fred, to "step in and take over," whether or not circumstances warranted the intervention. She naturally "stepped in" and "managed," that is, mistreated her own organs whenever she was tortured by her symptoms. Then she "took over" both in the matter of self-diagnosing and self-treatment, perennially "fighting" her sleeplessness and fatigue and working herself up over her palpitations and head pressures. That she "tried the hardest" to throw off fears and obsessions was merely a rather insignificant part of the total picture.

Possessive wives and mothers, driven on by the mania for "taking over," may do great harm to their henpecked and hamstrung "dear ones." The children may become warped and the husbands alienated by the exaggerated and unnecessary solicitude. But when patients bring their "stepping in" techniques to bear on their symptoms, resorting to self-diagnosing and self-treating, the results are bound to be disastrous. They become self-conscious, the one about his heart, the other about his digestion or elimination, a third about some paltry defect of memory and attention. Then they conceive all manner of suspicions about the possibility of grisly diseases, cancer, hypertension, coronary failure, arthritis and what not. If this happens, the patients become morbidly introspective, take notice of every trifling reaction and go into wild hysterics over a "skipped heart beat," an itch in the rectum, a streak of blood in the stools, or over a mythical swelling under the skin. A crack in a joint throws them into jitters, a cough drives them frantic, a muscle pain in the left chest conjures up the specter of a coronary thrombosis, and the now famous lump in the breast means cancer, of course. Reckless self-diagnosing of this kind is the most vicious sort of sabotage. I hope that, in the future, when the itch to "step in and take over" tickles you again, you will refuse to heed it and will, instead, step aside and let me take over—the diagnostic function.

DR. LOW'S COLUMN
SOME FACTS THE DENTIST OUGHT TO KNOW ABOUT HIMSELF*

A patient consulting you complains of a disorder affecting the organs of his mouth, usually his teeth. He asks you to put his teeth in order. This is a matter of professional skill and technical efficiency which I am ill equipped to discuss. There is, however, one facet of the dentist-patient relationship which is identical with or similar to the one encountered in the medical field, particularly in psychiatric practice, that is, the patient's personality or his Self. The problems of the Self, whether it be that of the patient or the dentist, ought to be considered the proper area on which the psychiatrist can venture his interpretive acumen.

It is a truism but must be stated because it is likely to be forgotten that the patient is not only the owner of teeth but also the possessor of a Self. That Self may be disordered as much as are his teeth. This being the case, the dentist or anybody who treats sufferers, will have to acquire a satisfactory knowledge of what Selves are, how they come to be disordered and how they can be put in order again.

We will all agree that disorder can be brought about by sickness, death, economic calamity and social distress. But it is not very probable that, while working on your patient, you will choose to discuss weighty issues of this kind. The greater likelihood is that the conversational fare which you will select will touch on everyday events, on babies and golf and baseball and topics of a similar lightweight character. In other words, you will chat. While chatting, you will report facts and experiences, for instance, the fact that you played a grand game of golf yesterday or the glorious experience of being the proud father of a strapping, athletic youngster of 8½ pounds. A factual report of this sort can hardly be expected to wound the sensibilities of the listener or to throw his feelings out of order. Suppose, however, that in the course of this innocent chat you spend fully half an hour describing the little antics of the newborn baby; suppose, you go into a lengthy, detailed and unnecessarily repetitious account of how the baby smiles and kicks and yells, how expressive are his features, how he

*Paper read, February 6, 1952, by invitation from the Chicago Dental Society, at its 1952 Annual Midwinter Meeting.

moves with infinite grace and how his actions give unquestioned evidence of intelligent endowment; suppose you go on raving in this manner on the rare virtues of the tot, then, you did not speak of facts and experiences but treated your patient to a tiresome recital of *your* views about *your* son. The disproportionate length with which you dwelt on the details of your description demonstrated that you hold an extravagant opinion of the importance of your own Self. You assumed that what touches *you* deepest must also be of deepest concern to others, that *your* boundless delight with your son must be shared by your auditors and that what is vital to *you* must be just as vital to them. If your behavior was as I described, your patient will draw the conclusion, intuitively or reflectively, that you consider your own Self as very important and the Selves of others as less important or not important at all. He will feel annoyed, bored, perhaps disgusted. And annoyance, boredom and disgust we call *frustrating feelings*. And if you permit yourself to throw your listeners into a condition of frustrated feeling you cause an emotional disorder, perhaps one of brief duration, but a disorder, nevertheless.

The emotional disorder of which I spoke was occasioned by your imprudent display of your sense of importance. That attitude of Self-importance is a *belief*, the belief that your own Self is singular, unique, outstanding, superior. Let me add that there is perhaps not one single intellectually alert individual walking this earth who does not subscribe to the illusion (belief) that his own Self has the qualities of singularity, uniqueness, superiority and outstanding ability. Nobody endowed with a modicum of push and ambition thinks of his own Self as being merely average, or as being unimportant. This refusal to face or admit one's basic limitations is what underlies the sense of Self-importance. And when two persons meet, the situation is one in which the sense of Self-importance of the one encounters the sense of Self-importance of the other.

I told you that Self-importance is a belief. Let me try to explain what precisely is here meant by the term "belief." If you say, "I believe," what you really wish to imply is that you do not know; that, instead, you merely believe; that what you believe is by no means certain knowledge; that it is nothing but an opinion which you hope to be true without, however, having any assurance that it is valid or proof against challenge. To express it differently: Belief is Doubt. If this be granted it ought to be obvious that if you hold the belief in the importance of your own Self, you doubt that importance at the same time. The trouble is that the belief in your importance gives you pleasure, that it raises the value of your ego, that it stimulates and exhilarates you. In other words, that belief is experienced by you as a *value*. True enough, that value is nothing but a vanity. But if a vanity is capable of providing pleasure and mental stimulation, it is not likely to be discarded. Instead, it will be sheltered, protected and defended against attack and challenge. And since the sense of importance is belief and doubt at the same time, it is almost certain to be challenged and questioned, if by nothing else, then, by the fact that somebody else makes a display of his own importance. This is the reason, I presume, why men and women of breeding hesitate to exhibit their own importance. They hesitate to challenge the vanities of others by displaying their own. They control the belief of their importance although they possess and value it.

We may now revert to the example which I quoted: You spoke of a baby, of its weight and strength, its lusty movements, good looks and intelligent features. Let us assume that when you enumerated the excellences of the baby you refrained from mentioning or even indicating your own excellence. Let us further assume that the words and sentences which you used during the entire length of your wearying description were wholly inoffensive, in fair taste and manipulated with average tact. If this is true, then, the vocabulary which you chose could not possibly have created any emotional disorder. Which means that, while telling your story, you kept a watchful eye on the wording and phrasing which you employed. If an improper expression happened to push to the fore you instantly "spotted" it as tactless or distasteful and refused it access to your speech organs. Everyone who has a claim to being well-mannered performs this task of *Self-spotting* with every word which he intends to utter in the context of an address or conversation. You did likewise and succeeded in choosing suitable words and sentences. But in another and very vital aspect of your speech your spotting effort failed you disastrously. You failed to spot the impropriety of taxing the attention and interest of your patient with a story which was too elaborate and too wearisome. You certainly failed to spot that, in so doing, you staged an unseemly display of the importance of your own Self.

If I speak to a person I use my words and sentences because I am *disposed* to use them. In the one discourse my disposition is to use popular language, in the other my language is technical. Sometimes my speech is matter-of-fact, pale and uninspiring, at other times it is animated, vigorous, lively. All of these are dispositions. But I enter into discussions and conversations not only with *dispositions* but also with *predispositions*. No matter which words and sentences I may be disposed to employ, I may express them with a predisposition to be either critical or generous, self-minded or group-minded, impatient or forbearing, temperamental or gentle, self-important or self-effacing, emotional or calm. If your predispositions tend in the direction of criticism, self-mindedness, impatience, temper, emotionalism and self-importance you will be certain to hurt feelings and to create emotional disorder in your listeners. You will now realize that if you wish to avoid causing ill-will and emotional disorder you will have to apply your spotting techniques to your predispositions rather than to your dispositions. A person of breeding has learned to spot his dispositions in proportion to the training he received in childhood and adulthood. But many men of commonly good manners have unfortunately neglected to acquire the proper spotting techniques for checking the above mentioned predispositions which can all be subsumed under the heading of an exaggerated sense of Self-importance. And if a person, be he dentist, physician, grocer or statesman, wishes to gain knowledge about his Self my advice will be that he learn to spot his sense of Self-importance, and to keep in mind that conversations, discussions and chats are verbal exercises in the course of which the sense of Self-importance of one individual meets with the identical sense of Self-importance of the other; that Self-importance is a deep-seated predisposition; that it bears constant watching and spotting, and that if not properly spotted it will break out and will wound feelings and create emotional disorder.

A few remarks yet about "spotting." You know the phrase "to spot somebody in a crowd." Ordinarily, a single man is lost in a crowd. He is hidden from sight, obscured by the multitude. Once you have sighted him he is spotted. His identity is now clearly discerned and sorted out from the mass. In other words, spotting means to bring into plain sight what has been invisible or obscured.

The significance of every sentence or statement is or may be hidden in a welter of meanings. So is or may be every act. Suppose you ask a stranger for directions, and he says, "I am headed for the same locality and if you don't mind I'll walk with you." What this action and statement of the stranger may mean is not immediately apparent. The man may be disposed to be courteous and helpful. This would be fellowship. Or, he may be lonesome and eager for your company. This would be legitimate self-interest. Or, he may be a crook preying on unsuspecting victims. This would be criminality. If the man has a suave manner and appealing looks it will be difficult to spot the true meaning of his reaction. The example illustrates the fact that pragmatic acts and verbal communications are apt to be embedded in a multiplicity of meanings, each of which must be spotted in order to be identified properly.

Whether the man whom you accosted on the street acted from motives of fellowship or self-interest or criminality, in any of these cases he might have responded to your question with the friendly and reassuring phrase, "...if you don't mind I'll walk with you." Which means that one and the same *verbal expression* can be made to cover diverse mutually contradictory *inner experiences*. Even with the crook, the verbal expression could have been that of fellowship while at the same time his inner experience would have been that of criminality. If this is so, how can we ever spot the true and real meaning of an inner experience if we are offered nothing but its outer verbal expression? Here we strike against the problem of "truth" and "reality," and you will realize that, in actual life, it is of the utmost importance to be able to spot the "true" significance of a situation and the "real" intention of a person when we have nothing more substantial to go by than a verbal pronouncement.

This very vexatious issue of the "true" and "real" experience versus the dubious verbal expression points up the chief difficulty which the psychiatrist encounters in dealing with the complaint of a patient. Let me quote three simple examples which, I trust, will clarify the situation. A woman patient, cooperative and reasonably honest, complains that she cannot sit quietly for even two or three minutes. She becomes restless, "edgy" and has to jump from the chair and pace the floor.

Another patient is plagued by a voracious appetite accompanied by severe hunger-pains. A third claims she cannot fall asleep, "lately not even with pills." For the psychiatrist, statements of this kind carry the obligation to diagnose the "true" and "real" nature of the underlying disturbance, that is, to spot the inner experience on which the verbal expression (complaint) is based. Are the extreme restlessness of the first patient, the voracious appetite plus hunger-pains of the second, and the insomnia of the third the result of a physiological or of a psychological experience? Physiological disturbances (organic diseases) are "true" and "real" happenings, of course. They are not the result of mere belief, imagination and interpretation. And restlessness, sleeplessness and voraciousness are frequently due to organic disturbances. Sleep can be interfered with by a "true" experience of toxicity; a voracious appetite may be the organic expression of a "real" diabetes, and restlessness may be the early sign of an "actual" infection. On the other hand, any of these symptoms may be the outcome of such purely psychological elements as worry, anxiety and preoccupation. If they are, then, the conditions of restlessness, voraciousness and sleeplessness were not physiologically experienced but psychologically feared, worried about and anxiously anticipated. How, then, can the psychiatrist be certain, apart from a thorough physical and laboratory examination, whether the patient's complaints are based on "true" organic experiences or on mere psychological attitudes? The answer is: through a diagnostic method which will spot what in the verbal expression of the patient contradicts the supposed (and perhaps merely imagined) organic experience. I shall then ask the lady who was certain she could not sit quietly for even two or three minutes what she did when she had to wait one full hour in my waiting room. If I obtain the information that she kept her seat during the entire waiting period, my conclusion will be that what she did in my office she could have done just as well in her home; that if the restlessness was caused by an infection there was no earthly reason why the infectious process should suddenly and miraculously be shut off in my waiting room. "True" organic experiences do not shrewdly choose the precise locality where they wish to operate. And if a reaction is "choosy," its arbitrariness demonstrates that it contains an element which can arbitrarily choose between one location in which it will consent to appear and another in which it will prefer not to appear. And an element which has the power to select and choose and prefer is psychological, of course.

I shall now apply the same technique of spotting to the two other complaints which I mentioned. You remember that the one patient had a voracious appetite attended by hunger-pains. She was asked: Do you eat voraciously when you are in a movie, or when you visit friends? The answer was "no" which indicated that the symptom was selective and choosey, hence, psychological. The third patient, you will likewise recall, suffered from an insomnia which was so severe that it no longer responded to sedatives. After proper questioning the patient obliged with the following confession: "I can sleep when I ride in the bus; I have no trouble snoozing off in the beauty shop under the drier, and in your waiting room all I have to do is to sit down and I fall asleep, but at home I can't sleep. Isn't that funny?" Needless to say, this precise discrimination between the home in which the symptom of sleeplessness "agreed" to appear and the other places in which it chose to absent itself was not funny at all. It was an arbitrary, "choosy" manifestation and not a "true" organic experience of sleeplessness. I hope I was able to demonstrate to you that with a proper diagnostic procedure symptoms can be spotted as to whether they represent an organic experience or a functional one. If this is done the diagnostic "truth" stands revealed.

I should like to tell you in greater detail how patients can be trained to do their own diagnostic spotting; I should also be delighted to indicate to you how proper spotting can be successfully taught with regard to communication and conversation practiced in the daily routine of ordinary people who lack the doubtful distinction of being nervous patients; I should consider it a rare privilege, indeed, to be able to demonstrate to you how reading of newspapers and books or listening to the radio could be developed into an exquisite art of spotting the obscurities and inadequacies of what is offered to the eyes of the reader and the ears of the listener. But time does not permit to even mention the vast potentialities which this unlimited field opens to the teacher of spotting techniques.

In conclusion let me revert to the subjects of disposition and predisposition which I discussed above. The average person is not critical, that is, he is not disposed to fatigue himself with the exacting task of spotting. Should he wish to be trained in this difficult art he would have to acquire not only temporary dispositions to exercise it but a lasting predisposition for continuous spotting. This would call for persistent application and laborious practice. An enduring predisposition for correct spotting would save a person from becoming the dupe of his own personal prejudices or the fertile soil for appealing ideologies or a soft touch for persuasive sharpers. Should this spotting ideal ever materialize, millennium would be at hand, and I for one cannot be duped into the belief that millennium is around the corner or even a likely prospect for a far distant future.

QUOTATIONS FROM DR. LOW'S ADDRESSES

1. *Tenseness and Self-Consciousness*

The patient was in a depression of moderate intensity. He suffered but stayed on the job and performed satisfactorily. In spite of that he feared he was going to lose his position. "I am so tense," he complained, "that the men in the shop notice it. I have such difficulty concentrating that I hear only half of what they say. I am sure they notice it; they can't help noticing." I tried to explain to the man that tenseness is essentially an inner process, and that concentration is an activity that goes on inside the brain; that if he thinks that plain people can see or notice what goes on within him he credits them with extraordinary powers of penetration. My argument fell flat. The patient was not at all impressed. Presumably, he thought little of my powers of penetration. "Maybe you are right," he said politely, "people may not be able to look through me, but they certainly see the tenseness in my features. And they see the mistakes I make. The other day when the boss asked me something, I fumbled and took too much time to give an answer. Doesn't that prove to him that there is something wrong with my concentration?"

After listening to a patient who tells me a story of this kind, I usually say: "suppose it is true that people notice your tenseness or your difficulty of concentrating, what of it?" The patient is likely to reply, "Well, they know then that I am no good; they know there is something wrong with my nerves or my mind." Which reminds me that I have treated nervous and mental patients for upward of thirty years, and that to this very day, when a new patient enters my examining room, in the company of a relative or friend, I usually have to ask: "Who is the patient?" I have to do that most of the time unless the condition is so conspicuously nervous or mental that even the policeman on the corner could make the diagnosis. This indicates that, unlike the shop worker, I have not yet learned the mysterious art of looking at the face and making the diagnosis. This, I am certain, I shall never learn.

At times I see acquaintances, friends or neighbors who exhibit undoubted signs of severe tenseness and faulty concentration. But that does not by any means suggest to me that they are "no good," or that something is wrong with their "nerves or minds." I merely conclude that the person opposite me is just now ill-disposed, or that he happens to be preoccupied with the thought of a sick child at home, or that he has suffered business reverses, or received a notice of eviction or was served with a ticket for a traffic offense. This is what comes to my mind when I meet a person who is disturbed, and in consequence, looks tense. You may be certain that people in general do the same. Beholding a tense individual, they infer that a child is sick, or that business is poor, or that some other circumstances prevail in which environment is troublesome and fate unkind. Both they and I are inclined to place the responsibility for tenseness at the doorsteps of outer, environmental disturbances, not of inner, psychological maladjustment. This is the reason why when you complain of being edgy or restless, slowed down or worn out, the average person will advise you that what you need is a "change of environment." Unless he is a rank intellectualist, he is not likely to say that what you need is a psychiatrist. If you keep in mind this general tendency to blame tenseness on environmental difficulties, and not on a psychological imbalance you will stop worrying about "what people will think" when your features express tenseness. They will notice the tenseness and will think of your environment, not of your inner life. If you do that, you may yet be and remain tense, but you will no longer be self-conscious about the tenseness.

2. The Shame of Sabotage

"Yesterday," a patient said, "while I lay in bed my right leg suddenly became paralyzed." I asked, "were you able to move the leg?" The answer was, "Yes, but it cramped." And another patient exclaimed with heat, "I throw up all the time. I don't understand why I should always have to vomit." When questioned how often she had thrown up that day she replied, "Once today." She was then asked, "How frequently have you vomited yesterday?" The answer was; "I don't remember whether I threw up yesterday," I continued: "If you do vomit what comes up?" The patient, irritated, snapped back: "Well, doctor, maybe I don't throw up. But I feel like vomiting, and I am always nauseated and belching.''

In these two instances which could be multiplied hundreds of times, the one patient had a cramp and diagnosed a paralysis; the other had nausea and belching and termed it (diagnosed) ceaseless vomiting. You will understand that these two patients confused common and average disturbances (cramps, nausea and belching) with dangerous emergencies (paralysis and continuous vomiting). I want you to consider the details of the brief interviews I had with the two who were complainers rather than sufferers. When I asked the "paralytic" woman whether her leg could be moved she admitted naively, "Yes, but it cramped." She could not have supplied the information that the "paralyzed" leg moved unless she had tried and noticed that it did move. But if she knew that the leg had motion, why did she call it a paralysis? The answer is one with which you are familiar: patients love to exaggerate. They are eager to be rated as a severe case, not just a "case of nerves." They are confirmed romanto-intellectualists who want their condition to appear singular and extraordinary and not "just a common and ordinary nerve trouble." We call that sabotage which means that the patient refuses to accept the physician's diagnosis. All of this is plain and well known to you. But if I tell patients of this sort that they do not want to get well, they feel provoked and cry out, with a slightly faked indignation, "How can you say that I don't want to get well? Do I want to suffer?" My retort usually is: "I am certain you do not want to suffer, but neither do you want to do those things which will relieve your suffering. You do not want to bear your discomfort patiently and you hate (do not want) to accept my diagnosis of a 'merely' nervous condition, and you refuse (do not want) to control your temper, and you loathe to be told to use your muscles for the purpose of getting well. What you love (want to do) is to rant and complain and, through this, to whip up and perpetuate your symptoms. I agree that you would like to get well, but you do not want to do the things that must be done in order to get well.''

Clearly, the patient who diagnosed a crippling paralysis could have prevented her panic with the greatest ease. All she had to do was to notice the cramping of the leg (which she did) and to call it by its proper name: cramp. And the other patient could, likewise, have observed the occasional nausea and belching (which she did) and used the words "nausea" and "belching" instead of the terrifying phrase "I always vomit." If they failed to do that simple thing for the purpose of aiding their health, they were guilty of an offense which I call sabotage. They wanted sabotage and not health, that means, they did not want to get well.

An example which shows, in its inspiring simplicity, how sabotage of this kind can be avoided, was furnished at a recent Saturday panel by Frances. She reported how once, in a severe setback, she felt so exhausted that she could not lift her baby. "I got panicky," she said, "and suddenly I dashed out of the house and ran to my sister who lives several blocks away. Then it occurred to me that if I could make that dash to my sister I could have certainly picked up my baby. That made me feel ashamed of myself. I realized I had sabotaged shamefully, and the shame of it made me decide to drop my sabotaging for good. I did and have had no panic since." What a shame that so many of my patients sabotage but do not feel the shame of it.

3. The Patient Is an Apprentice, Not a Master

"I had four good days," said the patient, "but today, oh, palpitations and head pressures and dizziness and sweats, and I am so restless that I can't sit still a minute. It's always the same story: I improve for a few days and then flop again." Ida—that's the patient's name—continued her hysterical recital of woes and pains and sufferings, finally winding up with the statement, "Honestly, I can't see how I can ever get well if I always slip back after I have had the slightest improvement."

This story of improvement followed by a setback is nothing new to my patients. It ought to be no news to anybody who has studied my writings in which I have stressed page after page that setbacks after improvements are inevitable. If they are inevitable, they ought to be expected; and if my patients expected them they would not be scared into hysterias and despair. Ida was duly warned that setbacks cannot be avoided, but when a setback materialized she was stunned and drifted into a panic.

In order to get well a patient must practice. This means that he must make up his mind to become an apprentice. After an apprentice has been shown how to do a certain job, he is naturally expected to make mistakes. He cannot possibly hope to acquire mastery after the first or second trial, not even after dozens of trials. He will have to try and fail, try again and fail again, and will be asked by his master to continue the method of trial and failure till proper experience and assurance will have been secured. The more he fails the better he will learn till finally, after endless attempts and frustrations, he will achieve mastery.

My patients apprentice themselves to me but want to obtain mastery after a few initial trials. Ida had four good days which was nothing short of a triumph in the early stage of her apprenticeship. Had she considered herself an apprentice she would have rejoiced at such a rapid progression. "Four solid days without gross failure," she should have told herself, "that proves that I am making headway. It shows that I am learning. Of course," she should have continued, "there will be days of failure, and plenty of them. But I shall expect the failures and will not let them discourage me." Had Ida done that she would have anticipated, with calm and determination, the failure (setback) of the fifth day with the result that the setback would not have been "worked up" to its hysterical fury. But Ida expected instant victory and early mastery. There is nothing more demoralizing than to expect victory and suffer defeat. More demoralizing yet is to gain an initial victory and to assume that now the war is won. The next defeat is certain to leave the fighter discouraged and to throw him into despair. The cardinal mistake which Ida made was that she thought the war against her illness was over because she had scored an initial victory of four days of freedom from symptoms. The subsequent, unavoidable defeat sapped her courage and weakened her spirit. She was demoralized because of her extravagant and unwarranted expectations.

My patients will have to learn that nervous symptoms have formidable strength; that the task of conquering them calls for a long-drawn-out battle, and that in order to score a final victory over a well entrenched enemy it is necessary to be prepared for a protracted struggle in which defeats will follow upon initial successes. If the patients want to gain mastery and win the final battle of this fierce struggle they will have to be ready to engage in a course of apprenticeship which will last months and, in rare cases, years. During this period of training a series of recurring failures and defeats will have to be wisely expected and patiently borne. If you are fully prepared for defeats, the recurrence of a setback will not terrify you. You will face it with the knowledge that, after all, you are merely a fledgling apprentice who, in his forward march toward mastery, must anticipate temporary failure before final mastery will be achieved.

DR. LOW'S COLUMN

1. POSSIBILITIES AND PROBABILITIES. HOW TO SPOT THEM.

Alma, her husband and their two children had just moved to a suburb and were delighted with the attractive appearance of the new home. After two weeks Alma was seized with the fear that the railroad tracks, two blocks from the house, might be a danger to the children. She tried to "fight off" the thought but "had no luck" and decided to consult me at my office. When I saw her she was in a setback with head pressures, poor sleep, scant appetite and lowered spontaneity. She feared she was in for another period of hospitalization. "You can't call that a silly fear," she exclaimed with half-stifled sobs, "Couldn't the children stray from the house and walk on the tracks? I just shudder to think what could happen." After a brief session Alma realized that it was all sabotage and emotional processing (working self up) and dismissed the fears in a short time.

Why did Alma have to seek my help? Why did she fail to practice self-help? Her attendance at classes had been almost continuous for two years. Her participation in the activities of her local family group had been regular and fruitful. She had on numerous occasions advised and comforted other patients, had taught them how to practice our spotting techniques. Her panel examples were well nigh faultless, her knowledge of "Mental Health" nothing short of exemplary. With such a record of understanding and skill of foreign spotting, why did she neglect the spotting of her own experiences, that is, self-spotting? It would have been easy for her to surmise that the fear for the children's safety was a gross instance of exceptionality. There are many children in her present neighborhood. And Alma knew that her neighbors did not, on an average, go into hysterics at the thought of the railroad tracks. Why did she hold the notion that her own role as a mother was singular and exceptional and totally different from that of the average mother? She knew of no case of a neighbor's child having ever been injured by a train. If so, why did she assume that her children would be the only exception? Clearly, Alma could have spotted her fear as stemming from the idea of exceptionality but refrained from doing so because the proper spotting would have reminded her of something she did not care to know: that she was nothing but an average mother and average person. And people in general, not only patients, hate to be rated or rate themselves as "nothing but average."

Alma suffered from two different conditions, (1) her depression, (2) the thought of danger to the children. At the time I saw her she made scant mention of her depression. "I don't worry about my symptoms," she said, "I can handle them. I know they are merely distressing and not dangerous. What worries me are my children, not my symptoms." That was an excellent distinction between inner dangers and outer dangers. It demonstrated that my patients have learned to spot symptoms and, through the spotting, to dispose of them. But it is precisely Alma's experience which points up the need for teaching patients how to spot outer dangers. In her case, the outer danger impressed her as a "realistic" worry about the security of the children. She was their mother, and if danger threatened, she could not afford to take risks. How is a mother to know what, in her children's lives, is dangerous and what harmless?

How is she to do her maternal spotting? You may be inclined to say that the function of Recovery is to train patients for the task of controlling symptoms and not mothers for the job of child-care. That would be a short-sighted view. Many of our patients are mothers, and if they do not know how to avoid unnecessary worry their nerves will suffer. Fortunately, our spotting techniques are sufficiently broad and comprehensive to apply to fields which have little to do with symptoms. They cover a vast stretch of everyday life, particularly the everyday reactions of mothers. Alma, in her perplexity, asked: "Couldn't the children stray from the house and walk on the tracks?" They could, no doubt. But they could also set the house on fire and could swallow some poisonous substance and could fall from a third story window. And if you say that somebody "could," the phrase points to a mere *possibility,* not to a *probability,* assuredly not to a *certainty.* To base conclusions and expectations on bare possibilities is to lack a sense of realities. If you wish to worry about empty possibilities, well, there are very few things in this world of ours which are not possible. Possible dangers are about as many as there are seconds and minutes in one's daily life. And to worry about possibilities is—unrealistic. That's what mothers, and people in general, are who work themselves up about possible dangers. They are unrealistic.

It is true that if a mother is entrused with the care of a tiny infant, she will have to be on the alert against sheer possibilities. With a baby everything is possible, and every possibility may turn at any time into a dangerous probability or tragic certainty. But as the child grows into the years of school age, the dangerous possibilities diminish until they reach an average minimum. This is the period in which mothers have to learn how to distinguish between possible and probable dangers. Which brings us back to our basic differentiation between exceptionality and averageness. Average people may worry about possibilities but they do not work themselves up over them into anxieties and panics. And the best advice I can give mothers who are in doubt as to the harmfulness or harmlessness of an outer objective situation, is to ask the simple question: Do my neighbors, friends and relatives, on an average, fear the things that frighten me? If the answer is "no," the decision can be made that the situation is of average harmlessness. The fear can then be dropped. You see here that the spotting of objective, outer conditions is just as feasible as, and somewhat more simple than the spotting of subjective, inner conditions.

2. THE DUAL AND DIVIDED WILL

Chester was "nose-conscious." For the past ten years he had patronized numerous nose and throat specialists who, with a singular unanimity of opinion, had invariably diagnosed the condition as nervous. This failed to satisfy the patient who insisted he "knew" it was an allergy (and not nerves) which rendered the nose hopelessly stopped-up and kept it lastingly out of function. His continuous sniffling was a source of irritation to the members of the family and earned him the reputation of an unmannered person among his friends and acquaintances. He had improved under office and class treatment, but the sniffling was still noticeable. He was asked, "why do you insist on keeping up this ugly habit?" Indignantly he shouted, "How can you say such a thing? Do I do it intentionally?" And another patient, Mae, witnessed a holdup from her window and instantly developed head pressures and violent palpitations which try as she might she "could not control." Four weeks after the holdup incident she was asked why she still insisted in working herself up over the experience. "Doctor," she exploded, "how can you say I insist on having my symptoms? Do you really believe I want my head to ache and my heart to pound?"

In spite of the energetic protests of the patients, I still maintain that Chester *wanted* to sniff and Mae *refused* to stop her pressures and palpitations. I maintain likewise that every nervous patient who does not improve in a reasonable period of time refuses to lose his symptoms and insists on keeping them alive, provided it is a patient who has gone through the Recovery training and has been taught the method of how symptoms can be spotted and stopped. In Chester's case the situation was clear: He was told by me and by other consultants that his condition was nervous but he clung to his own diagnosis of an allergy. And when he asked, "Do I do it intentionally?" I did not hesitate to reply, "Of course, you do it by intention. You refuse deliberately and intentionally to accept the correct diagnosis. What else can that be but a refusal to get well?" In Mae's case the circumstances were more complex. She suffered a scare which left her with head pressures and palpitations. Unlike Chester she did not diagnose the pressure, let me say, as due to a brain tumor; nor did she refer the palpitations to a heart ailment. What she did was to process her scare into a sustained panic without making an effort to spot it as temper. I have no doubt that both Chester and Mae wanted to get rid of their symptoms and the discomfort they caused. But they did not want and refused to use the methods of self-help they had learned in Recovery. Which means that they did not want to get well. And the methods taught in Recovery are of the simplest: spot and stop your temper and your self-diagnosing.

It happens to me that at times I seat myself at my desk and begin to write a letter. Then my eyes catch sight of a book, and I pick it up and read it. After I have finished reading I may have to leave, and there is no time to finish the letter. Did I, in this instance, *want* to write the letter or did I want to read the book? The answer is: I wanted both the writing and the reading but I preferred the reading. Which means that I made a choice, and choices, as you know, are made by the Will. In the case of the letter and the book I had two Wills. The one (to write the letter) was weak, the other (to read the book) was strong. The strong Will carried the day, and the weak Will yielded, refusing to assert itself. I wanted to read and to finish a letter at the same time which was impossible. Instead of willing one activity only at one time, I wanted both. My Will was divided, and it requires a *single, undivided Will* to carry through a job to its finish.

Those of my patients who are slow in improving suffer from a dual, divided Will. They want to get well but want it to come to them painlessly, without painful practice. They want health, but they do not want the discomfort of practicing rules and techniques. This means that they want and do not want. When Chester and Mae protested that they wanted health they were correct in the sense that they exercised a divided, dual Will. When I told them that they did not want health, I was equally correct in the sense that I expected them to apply themselves to the task with a single, undivided Will. My view of what a Will is supposed to be clashed with their views. The fact that they insisted on retaining their views stamped their behavior as sabotage. By sabotaging my views they sabotaged their own purpose of getting well.

DR. LOW'S COLUMN
I AM TIRED ALL THE TIME

Eleanor, in an outburst of temper, shouted: "Why is it that I can never relax? Will I always have to be so deadly tired?" I replied calmly, "You will be tired exactly as long as you will insist on working up your temper." Far from pacifying her, my explanation merely served to turn her excitement into a wild explosion. I sat looking at her with studied indifference. This seemed to puzzle her, and the puzzlement appeared to have a sedative effect. The result was that after a few minutes her yelling trailed down to a lower key. I then indicated that the interview was terminated and the next appointment was to take place two weeks hence. She snapped back, "I don't want a next appointment. I am tired of being bawled out each time I come to see you. When I leave your office I am just exhausted."

Eleanor had attended classes for close to two months, had read "Mental Health" and was tolerably acquainted with my views on temper as the main source of nervous fatigue. If she knew that her fatigue was due to temper, why did she refuse to curb her temperamental habits? You know the answer: temper is exciting and stimulating while self-control is a dragging, uninspiring, humorless practice. Temper is colorful and vitalizing while control is dull, wearisome and utterly lacking in glamor.

Like many other patients, Eleanor argued persuasively that her fatigue was of a genuine quality, a "real" fatigue. She was the mother of two children. "The youngsters are wild, they keep me busy all day. There is never a quiet moment day after day. They never give me a rest and, naturally, I am tired all the time."

This story about never getting a rest and, "naturally," being tired all the time is told by many mothers, patients or no patients. And I shall readily grant that a mother, being harassed by unruly children, has a right to be tired. But if a mother maintains that, "naturally," she is tired all the time, I shall question the justification of a tiredness which is present "all the time" and will seriously doubt the "naturalness" of a condition which conforms so little to nature that it actually defies it. By nature every fatigue yields to rest, and if a fatigue is there all the time, if it fails to yield to rest, then, emphatically, it is not at all natural but suspiciously artificial. That tiredness has been artificially created by a "worked up'' temper, and nature knows nothing of temper and very little if anything about the process of working oneself up.

There is much talk these days about the tired businessman. This modern creation voices the same inflated phrases which are used by the overworked mother. Like the modern mother the contemporary businessman is likely to complain that he "never" gets his rest and that, "naturally," he is tired "all the time." The remarkable thing is that while I frequently hear about the tired businessman, I do not remember having ever been told about the tired farmer or the tired laborer. You will easily guess the reason. The worker and farmer do an honest day of work, and their work is undoubtedly fatiguing. But after a suitable rest period they have regained their vitality and are, "naturally," no longer fatigued.

I shall try to outline the difference between the reactions of farmer and laborer, on the one hand, and those of modern mothers and present-day businessmen, on the other. The case of the modern mother is particularly instructive. This pathetic creature is continuously subjected, by professors of education and by writers or lecturers on child guidance, to a never ceasing torrent of advice on how to bring up children. The calamity is that these "scientists" have an exasperating habit of changing their views about every two years and not infrequently at shorter intervals. This alone is bound to throw the modern mother into chaos and confusion. Confusion becomes more confounded yet when the hapless mothers attend courses conducted successively by different lecturers, or if they read newspaper columns written by different authors. Since each lecturer or columnist has or may have a pet opinion of his own, the unwary readers or listeners are unhappily exposed to a multitude of views which may or do contradict one another. Chaos and confusion are then inescapable. The mothers become bewildered and unsure of themselves and do not know what to do and what to believe. The result is helplessness, sustained doubt and continued tenseness and strain. It is the strain of mental confusion which they then misinterpret as muscular fatigue. In actual fact, their fatigue is mental, not muscular. The mental fatigue, quite "naturally," does not yield to rest. Mothers of this kind, being eternally mystified and puzzled by the contradictory thoughts and views offered them by "trained experts," sense intuitively that the surest way to escape confusion is to stop thinking and viewing. Hence, they are afraid to take a rest. Resting means thinking, and thinking has, in our day of "expert" counseling, turned into strain and tenseness. The mothers conclude erroneously that they are tense and tired because they work too hard. The reverse is the truth. They force themselves to work hard because resting and thinking renders them mentally strained and nervously tired. The hard work is expected to rescue them from the ordeal of hard thinking.

The case of the tired businessman could be explained on a similar basis of confusion causing mental strain and nervous fatigue and then being misinterpreted as fatigue of the muscles. It could easily be demonstrated that modern businessmen, exactly like modern mothers, do not become tired because they work too hard but, on the contrary, work hard because they suffer from a mental strain which they try frantically to escape by working overtime. But the demonstration would call for a lengthy explanation which, I am afraid, will strain and tire you. I shall merely indicate that modern business is highly competitive and creates an exceeding measure of frustration, self-doubt and self-blame. The perpetual self-condemnation induces a high degree of mental strain and nervous fatigue. Laborers and farmers are spared the grind of fierce competition and manage to avoid or mitigate their quota of frustration, bewilderment and confusion. They work at least as hard as does the businessman but, avoiding ruinous competition and the conflicting views of "experts," they are under relatively little strain, hence, they dare to rest and are, "naturally," not tired "all the time."

DR. LOW'S COLUMN
THE WILL TO FEAR

Nick had been employed by a local bank and was to be promoted to the position of assistant cashier. When the president of the bank broached the news to him Nick was stunned. In the afternoon he felt apprehensive, and after retiring that night he was unable to sleep. Before long he drifted into a depression which had lasted three months when he consulted me. He was assigned to classes and recovered after several months of office and class treatment. The position of assistant cashier had been kept open for him. He accepted it fearlessly and performed skillfully.

Reactions of this kind in response to promotions are nothing unusual. I have encountered them in a considerable number of patients. The men and women who dread promotions are so-called perfectionists, and what they fear is the new or added responsibility. Given an opportunity to examine persons of this kind one discovers an all-pervasive disposition toward apprehensiveness which covers vast areas of the daily routine. There is the fear of speaking up, of meeting new people, of joining crowds; the fear of doing or having done harm to someone; the fear of having forgotten to lock the door; of having said the wrong thing or having run afoul of some trivial convention. Fear of something or other is written all over the face and mentality of these good souls who are forever steeped in a suspicion of their presumed propensity for evil.

During the first few weeks of treatment Nick made little progress. I tried to convince him that, having been for many years a capable and trusted employee of the bank, he could be depended on to do justice to his new responsibilities. But my eloquence was wasted. I ventured a reassuring opinion, and it was instantly brushed aside by the insistence that I did not know how stupid was his thinking and how unreliable his action. "I have always been dumb and irresponsible," he said, "but I covered up and got by. I know that in this new position I will be found out, and that will finish me and my family." I tried to disabuse him of this disastrous self-estimate, but my arguments were powerless against the force of his stubborn conviction. That conviction had hardened into an unshakable obsession that he was utterly lacking in capability and dependability.

All my patients suffer from obsessions which, in the beginning of treatment and training, have a fatal way of sidetracking judgment and common sense. In this initial stage of my curative effort the vast majority of the patients are fiercely addicted to and obsessed by rigid beliefs for which they fight with an almost perverse obstinacy. They believe and wage ferocious battles to prove that their sleeplessness is beyond hope, that their depressions are incurable or that the mythical damage which months of palpitations have inflicted on their hearts is irreparable. These obsessions are based on fears, and fears are nothing more than beliefs in impending danger. The question is: why do my patients hold on to their fearful beliefs with a determination which thwarts every attempt to change them? Beliefs can be altered and dropped at will. Why do my patients fail to use their Will for the purpose of discarding their fear beliefs? Why do they, instead muster all their willpower for an heroic effort to repulse me when I try to rid them of their fears, panics and anxieties? Do they want to preserve them? Do they *crave* to perpetuate them? Are they actuated by a mysterious WILL TO FEAR? If they are, what is the reason?

The answer is that fear, though tormenting and damaging to mental balance and physical welfare, is also a *value*. In its milder degrees, in the shape of worry, caution, circumspection, prudence and wariness, it is positively helpful in avoiding danger. In this sense, fear is a protection against hazard and misfortune. This aspect of fear as a beneficial and protective agent has been drummed and drilled into us day in and day out, minute after minute, when we were children. Our parents, mindful of their responsibilities, never tired warning us against the host of dangers which crowd the daily routine of everybody's activities. There were physical dangers in outer environment, and we were cautioned daily and hourly to "look out," to "watch" our steps, to "be careful." Our mothers wrapped us in an atmosphere of vigilance and apprehension lest we might hurt ourselves or bring ruin to things. Our attention was also forcefully and incessantly turned on the dire dangers of inner environment. We had to be on guard against our impulses to destroy objects, our inclination to be loud and boastful, and our tendency to be a nuisance to everybody and a comfort to no one. From early morning to late evening we were exposed to necessary and well-meaning sermons to curb our innate desires to neglect courtesy, our inclination to tell little lies and our impulse to snatch the possessions of other children. We were treated to never-ending preachments against laziness, disorderliness and neglectfulness. In all of this, the abiding impression which settled in our childish brains was that our desires, wishes and impulses were basically harmful and in constant need of watchfulness. In the end we acquired a view that danger lurked everywhere, outside and inside ourselves, and the companion view that the only thing that can save us from physical, social and moral ruin was the protective action of fear. Fear was thus raised to the level of a value. It was of value because it protected us from danger.

When we were children our feelings tended to be maximal and extreme. Our joys were explosive outbursts of rollicking mirth, our resentments were orgies of anger, and our fears were paroxysms of anxiety. Gradually, as we grew up, we learned the difference between those mild feelings which are beneficial and the excessive feelings which spell harm. In point of fear we learned that worry and caution, mild and useful, are desirable and valuable, while the wild anticipation of emergencies, far from rating as value, is actually in the nature of a vice. In this manner, we adjusted our apprehensions. We managed to be cautious always and fearful seldom. The sermons and preachments, painfully endured in our childhood, had crammed our brains with all manner of senseless fears, but as we grew to adulthood, the indiscriminate beliefs in danger gave way to balanced judgment and mature discrimination.

Nick failed to grow up with regard to his views about outer and inner environment. He did not mature prior to his Recovery training and looked on all his impulses and feelings as invariably harmful and on *all* events of outer environment as potentially treacherous. A promotion was conceived by him as a threat. His impulses and desires, it seemed to him, threatened to approach the new task with a defective sense of responsibility.

His coworkers and superiors were likewise viewed as a threat because they were ''certain'' to discover his basic incapacity and unreliability. The only thing that appeared likely to protect against these dangers was continuous, unrelenting fear. To his mind, fear, unwavering fear, possessed the quality of a powerful protective device. As such, it had to be maintained and defended and never lost sight of. When he consulted me it was clear that he could not be cured unless he was made to spot his panics as what they were: an instrument of protection, planted in his childish brain by parents alive to their parental duties but destined to be given up in adulthood when the mind unfolded and judgment ripened. Prior to his Recovery training he had failed to realize that devices and tools must be used with discrimination. Soon he learned that what must be discriminated were: mild cautions, on the one hand, which are beneficial and valuable, and severe fears, on the other, which are harmful and the very reverse of a value. Our spotting techniques gave him the means of approaching the inner and outer dangers with a mature, discriminating view. After acquiring a reasonable facility with the spotting art he entered a process of late maturation and discarded the WILL TO FEAR.

DR. LOW'S COMMENTS ON EXAMPLES OF RECOVERY PRACTICE

EXAMPLES OF RECOVERY PRACTICE, JUNE 1952

1. Denver, Colorado—Sherley M.
[Courage, Will and Determination]

An example contained in a letter from Sherley M., of Denver, to Treasure R., leader of Brighton Branch—

Dear Treasure:

A lady called me last Wednesday to tell me that if I wanted my daughter, Jill, to be a "Brownie," I would have to attend an organization meeting of 22 mothers on Friday morning. After receiving the call I felt very low. It always makes me so uncomfortable when there is something that I would like to do for the children that I'm afraid I can't do. And Jill is so anxious to be a "Brownie." I kept thinking, "Oh, if I could only go." I wanted so badly to talk to you, Treasure, but then I knew what you would say—that I'd have to stop working myself up about it, that everybody has sensations.

Then on Thursday evening we had a Recovery home meeting at our house, which made me feel further encouraged. Friday morning I made up my mind to make my muscles work toward getting ready to go to the "mothers-of-Brownies" meeting. I sent Jill off to school, took Susan, my younger daughter, to a neighbor's and went. I realized then that I would be all right when I found I wasn't irritable or tense at all but was actually singing!

It all turned out fine. I wasn't absolutely comfortable but I don't imagine the others were either—meeting all those new people. I didn't have a sign of the old panic. I knew that I wasn't ready to volunteer as a leader of their organization but I offered to baby-sit for the leader, do the telephoning, and drive the children around when they wanted me to. I know that all of this is going to lead to a good many meetings, etc., but somehow I'll take these things as they come.

I'm to take Jill to another mother-daughter meeting of the "Brownies" soon. Yes, I'm scared but I'm going anyway.

P.S. I went to another meeting of the "Brownies." Found myself helping with everything and—no tenseness. Feel like life is once more a wonderful thing.

Sincerely,
Sherley

Dr. Low's Comment:

The phrase "I'm scared but I am going anyway" expresses beautifully the very core of Recovery thinking. It is a veritable declaration of independence from sensations, symptoms and panics and a firm determination to let no scares interfere with the realistic business of daily life. Ignoring fears and moving muscles is the essence of courage, will and determination, which means the essence of Recovery thinking.

2. *Chicago, Illinois—Frank R.*
[Courage to Make Mistakes]

Frank R.:

One Saturday last fall I had occasion to go to the Union Station after the Saturday meeting. Harriette and I were going out of town to visit her parents. As Harriette was working I was to meet her at the station before train time.

I left the Recovery office around five o'clock which was plenty early as the train didn't leave until six. I walked over to the bus stop to get the Jackson Blvd. bus. I expected one to arrive in a very few minutes. A number of buses passed and I was beginning to get a little anxious and tense. I still had plenty of time but it was growing shorter. Then I started looking toward Michigan Blvd. where the bus should turn from the South. I noticed that numerous buses passed along the Boulevard but none of them turned, all continued going North. The endless procession of North side buses went on. Now twenty minutes had passed and I really was worried because my time was running short. I began to think I would take a cab. Just then a person who had also been waiting for a bus for some time came up to me and asked me what bus I was waiting for. I said, "I am waiting for the #26 Jackson Blvd. bus." This stranger said, "If I am not mistaken I believe that that bus turns on Jackson Blvd." I was dumbfounded. Here I, a man who has lived in Chicago for 35 years, had waited a half hour on Adams for the Jackson bus.

By the time the stranger had straightened me out there was so little time left that I scurried about and got a cab. I was too taken up with this business to notice any symptoms but a couple of minutes later when I was seated in the cab I noticed them. I was extremely tense and was sitting on the edge of my seat, my stomach was knotted up, I was so disgusted with myself that I almost felt like crying, I had an acute headache and my vision was blurred. A few minutes before I had been in good spirits and now I was deeply depressed. I kept thinking, over and over to myself how stupid I had been, not knowing the difference between Adams and Jackson after 35 years.

More symptoms developed. I got chest pressures and numbness in my legs, and my thoughts were racing a mile a minute.

Soon I spotted what I was doing. I was working myself up by continuously blaming myself and by dwelling on the fact that I had stood on the wrong corner. I decided that the working up process had to stop. I remembered that it is average to make mistakes. And that countless people must have waited on wrong corners as I had done. In fact, I then recalled that I had done the same thing several times before. I also recalled that on the train I ride every night it practically never fails that there isn't at least one person who has taken the wrong train by mistake. I began to relax, sat back on my seat and waited until we reached the station.

By the time I met Harriette at the station my symptoms had evaporated. I told her what had happened and she just laughed. Sometime later when we had returned from our trip I told several of the Recovery members about the incident. None of them seemed to regard the incident as a cataclysmic event. I later told a fellow at work and he didn't seem a bit astonished either.

Before I had my Recovery training the fear of making mistakes was, with me, the preoccupation of my every waking moment. It was an obsession with me, my every waking moment was devoted to past, present and future mistakes. I ate, slept and breathed mistakes. The result of this never ending preoccupation with mistakes were constant symptoms such as: poor sleep; poor appetite; fatigue; depression; my thoughts were the dreariest and most pessimistic kind; palpitations; tremors, night sweats; confusion; indecision; self-disgust; lack of self-confidence and constant tenseness. Today I get symptoms but spot and stop them quickly. I can do that now because in Recovery I have learned to have the COURAGE TO MAKE MISTAKES in the trivialities of daily life.

Dr. Low's Comment:

After reading Frank's example Dr. Low declared that Frank gave such an excellent description of his sabotaging and subsequent spotting and self-control that no further comment seems to be called for.

3. Evansville, Indiana—Florence L.
[Exceptionality and Averageness]

Margaret V., leader of the Evansville branch, gave a talk to a group of people the other evening about Recovery. She read bits from "Predisposition, Partnership, and Partisanship" and "The Courage to Make Mistakes." A lively discussion followed and many said that they had had nervous difficulty and they thought that Dr. Low's book would be of help to them.

Three of those who were at this meeting came to our next Recovery meeting—where there were also three other newcomers—making a total of 16 people attending. Florence L., who is relatively new herself, gave some very helpful hints to those who were attending for the first time.

Florence L.:

"When I was first contacted by Evansville members I made excuses and then said to my husband, "Well, I didn't get anything out of that." But my husband told me he thought I ought to go to the meetings. So the next time I went and I thought at the time of the meeting that I didn't want to go back again because it didn't seem that there was anything in it that applied to me. But the next time I went again anyway and now I can't wait until the next meeting comes. So don't stay away after one meeting just because you think it isn't for you. Come again anyway and soon you will see how much it helps you."

If a patient, attending a panel meeting, has the impression that he or she does not "get anything out of that," that means that his or hers is considered to be a "different case." In my more than thirty years of intensive experience with patients I have met nothing but average cases. In all of them I have observed the following pattern. There are the average run of symptoms which are due to average type of tenseness, and the tenseness is created or maintained by either temper or self-diagnosing or by both. And the average patient can easily discover within himself both temper and self-diagnosing. A patient, prior to being exposed to Recovery training, hates to think of his Self or his case as average. To think of himself as "nothing but average" means to give up the vanity and glamour of fancying oneself as "singular," "different,' "exceptional." It means to forego the exhilarating feeling of being important.

4. Brighton, Michigan—Mary Aice L.
[Sense of Humor]

Mary Alice L.—

Mary Alice is one of our newer members but she gave this excellent example of Recovery practice:

Knowing that she was going to have company at the end of the week, she decided not to leave all the cleaning until the last minute but to do a little each day so she wouldn't have to rush around and make herself tense just before the company arrived. This alone is good stiff Recovery practice for Mary Alice. Each day she slowly but surely accomplished what she had planned and by Friday she had the place ready except for a last minute dusting.

Saturday morning she was surprised to hear her husband say that some men were coming in to wash her kitchen and bathroom walls. Her first impulse was to sit down and cry but no sooner was the thought, "I'm going to cry," born than Mary Alice spotted that she was dramatizing. She took one last look at her mirror-like kitchen floor with its three coats of carefully applied wax, thought of the extra work she would have to do cleaning up after the men, and of the necessary extra work she would have to do washing the curtains to match the washed walls. Then, as you might imagine she would, she indulged in a bit of temper display with her well-meaning husband.

But the more she talked, in temper, the more she could feel her symptoms coming on until finally she stopped short and realized how trivial was the issue of washed kitchen walls in comparison with the all important consideration of her health. Later, however, she had the temperamental thought that she would ask her mother-in-law who *she* thought was right and, she reflected—"If she says my husband is right I will know she's prejudiced." This idea, when she spotted it, was so funny to her that she had to tell her husband and they both had a good laugh over it.

Mary Alice realized that she had not handled the situation entirely without sabotage but felt that she had come a long way to be able to spot her dramatizing and taking herself too seriously. As a result of this much improved spotting she is feeling better all the time.

Dr. Low's Comment:

This is a very instructive example how the common frustrations of daily life can be borne and remedied by a sense of humor. It takes a sense of humor to think of one's self and one's frustrations as average. The philosophy of Recovery is opposed to the sense of self-improtance and favors the sense of group-importance. The knowledge that "I am not so important" creates a sense of humor.

EXAMPLES OF RECOVERY PRACTICE, AUGUST 1952

1. *Denver, Colorado—Kate S.*
[Tired of Pampering Symptoms]

Kate S.—

Kate, who fears crowds of people, has been making her muscles work by attending the dog races with her husband. The other night they were not able to get seats and Kate felt that she could never stand up for the whole evening. She had palpitations and felt sure she was going to faint. Then she realized that her symptoms were "distressing but not dangerous" and that nothing dreadful was going to happen. She even stood in line to place her husband's bets as further practice.

In pointing out how much she has changed since she started to practice Recovery, Kate mentioned that she is now tired of pampering her symptoms.

Dr. Low's Comment:

This example is succinct and meaty and requires no comment, except that I was intrigued by the exquisitely apt and striking expression that Kate "is now tired of pampering her symptoms." I take it that the phrase "I am tired" means "I am disgusted with" or "I have no further use for," and that the phrase "pampering symptoms" refers to the tendency to process a nervous complaint and to work it up to unrestrained emotionalism and boundless hysteria. All of it represents a refreshing sense of humor, because the essense of humor is not to take one's dear self too seriously. And if Kate is likely to call her past reactions by the name of "pampering symptoms" she gives every evidence that, at the very least, she can now view her past with a sense of humor. And if a person is ready to laugh at his or her past imbecilities, he or she can be depended on to make their humorous approach to their present imbecilities which, in the case of a nervous patient, mean sabotaging, self-diagnosing and self-pampering. The best cure for nervous symptoms is humor, that is, the refusal to take them seriously.

2. *Muscatine, Iowa—Charles F.*
[Symptoms and the Physician]

Charles F.—

Charles called one day to say that he had just experienced "double vision." He said that it lasted about five minutes. Prior to Recovery this experience would have alarmed him and he frequently did work himself up over this symptom. Now, he said: "I know when Dr. Low says it's 'distressing but not dangerous,' all I have to do is wait calmly and the discomfort will pass."

Dr. Low's Comment:

Charles states that he had double vision for five minutes. He adds that "Dr. Low says" about nervous symptoms that they are "distressing but not dangerous." And thinking about this dictum of mine Charles concluded that double vision belongs in the same category of experiences which are "distressing but not dangerous." Well, Charles, the fact that your double vision disappeared in five minutes indicates that it was not dangerous. But I shall advise you to have yourself reexamined if ever you experience again that thing which you call "double vision." It is about the reverse of a nervous symptom. It is not distressing but has a way of being quite dangerous. At any rate, it calls for reexamination.

3. *Muscatine, Iowa—Vivian N.*
[Spotting and Muscle Control]

Vivian N.:

"Sunday morning when I woke up I noticed that a feeling of fatigue was immediately with me. Another symptom that I had was lack of appetite. With no desire to eat anything and a feeling of being all in I thought I'd just lie in bed a while. Then the thought struck me—this is sabotage. So I jumped out of bed and dressed, forced myself to eat breakfast and then went over and picked up my book, "Mental Health Through Will Training," and read the topic for our afternoon branch meeting—Will, Beliefs, and Muscles.

"Before I had finished reading the chapter my feeling of being all in had left. Prior to my Recovery training I used to give in to my symptoms and go back to bed. Now I can force myself to bear discomfort and, I might add, I am working regularly."

Dr. Low's Comment:

Vivian says: "Before I had finished reading . . . my feeling of being all in had left." This sounds like magic, and I do not wish Vivian or any of my patients to use the language of magic. Of course, Vivian never entertained the notion that reading a chapter of my book will do away with symptoms. Action only will do that, and action is either mental or muscular. The mental act *spots* your sabotaging (self-diagnosing and temper), and the muscular act *stops* the muscles from carrying out the sabotaging behavior. And casting a glance at what Vivian actually did, we find that prior to reading my book the thought struck her that "this is sabotage" (spotting) and she "jumped out of bed and dressed and forced herself to eat breakfast" (commanding the muscles). Do not misunderstand me as discouraging the reading of my book. I merely wanted to emphasize the surpassing importance of our two basic concepts of spotting and muscle control.

4. Brighton, Michigan—Mary Alice L.
[Spotting Temper and Commanding Muscles]

Mary Alice L.—
(Singing While You Work Technique)

In the past whenever Mary Alice started on her round of house keeping activities she would begin to feel ill. The dizziness she experienced when she tried to use the vacuum cleaner was so severe she had to hang on to the furniture and steady herself. She said she couldn't understand it because she thought she had her temper under control. She was told she was still full of temper and, in Mary Alice's own words:

"That made me mad when you told me I still had temper but I decided to try to spot it. The next morning I looked at the unmade beds and started throwing the covers up, mumbling under my breath, when it suddenly occurred to me that I certainly *was* full of temper. I realized that I rebelled against many things that were required of me as a wife and mother.

"The only thing I could think of to do to show good temper

control was to sing. So I began humming and before I knew it the beds were made. The vacuuming was next and I began that with the same method—humming a tune while I used the sweeper. To my amazement I didn't have to hang on to the furniture. Although I had a few sensations they were not severe and I found that my work was quickly done. I endorsed myself for doing it without temper.''

Mary Alice has applied the ''singing while you work'' method of becoming objective with great success but she realizes that the important thing was not the singing but rather the fact that she controlled her temper. The singing was simply proof that Recovery can be practiced happily and even joyfully.

Dr. Low's Comment:

What Mary Alice did was to sing a tune. This, she claims, fired her ambition to do and finish her household job which, prior to singing, dragged and crawled. Again I wish to state: This is magic, and in Recovery, we want to obtain results through hard work, not through easy maneuvers. No amount of singing or reading my book or listening to a panel or communicating with a Recovery veteran will be likedly to relieve a nervous patient of symptoms and suffering. The only thing that will accomplish that result is: spotting sabotage and commanding the muscles. That's what Mary Alice did: She spotted her reaction as temper, then commanded her muscles to make the beds. Incidentally, she sang or hummed which contributed to the final result, I am sure. But the singing or humming would have been futile had it not been preceded by proper spotting and adequate muscular action. You did an excellent piece of work, Mary Alice, but remember, the real feat you performed was the spotting and the use of your muscles. Your leader, Treasure, mentions that you realized that the main thing was not the singing but the control of temper.

5. Brighton, Michigan—Peggy N.
[Spotting and Control]

Peggy N.—

Peggy's 9 year old girl broke her collar bone and one afternoon Peggy put the tea kettle on to heat some water for the hot water bottle to try to make her daughter more comfortable. While it was heating Peggy lay down with her little girl and in a few minutes they were both sound asleep. When Peggy woke up she thought about the tea kettle. Flying to the kitchen she found the room white with steam and the kettle ruined. Peggy felt numb: What kind of a mother would fall asleep and neglect her injured child? What would her husband think?

Shocked as she was, she avoided, nevertheless, hysteria and wild processing. She knew that she must have the courage to make mistakes but she could not throw off remorse. Her sleep was scant and troubled that night and her thoughts went around and around that tea kettle. She was vaguely uncomfortable for several days until she finally calmed down.

Peggy said she could not understand why it took her so long to throw off the effects of this experience but through it all she realized that Recovery was helping her. Before Recovery she would have secretly bought a new tea kettle to keep the mistake from being noticed. As it was, she told the family and they didn't seem to think a thing about it. Different members of the group then recalled times when they had "burned" the roast to a crisp, broken dishes with careless use of heat, etc. The important thing was that Peggy knew that all she was suffering was discomfort and she was able, through her Recovery training, to prevent the vicious cycle from processing itself into a panic.

Dr. Low's Comment:

This example is very apropos and needs little or no comment, except for one remark contained in it. Peggy "could not understand why it took so long to throw off the effects of this experience..." My answer is: I don't understand it either. And let me tell you, Peggy, there are so many things I do not understand that it would be physically impossible to catalogue them. I do not understand why, on some mornings, I arise and find myself devoid of my customary energy, or why on some occasions I am sprightly and mentally alert and on other occasions my spirit seems to have gone from me and my disposition reaches a low ebb of dullness and indolence that is truly appalling. And I do not understand at all why if I have some unfathomable difficulty it lasts five minutes the one day and two or three hours the other. All of this is beyond my comprehension. Fortunately, it is immaterial whether a nervous condition is or is not understood. What counts is the knowledge that every nervous symptom, no matter how mysterious and incomprehensible, can be controlled through spotting thoughts and commanding muscles. You see, no matter what subject you patients will bring up, my answer is invariably and monotonously: Spot your thoughts and command your muscles!

1. *Chicago, Illinois—Phil C.*
[Self-Management and Self-Control]

Phil C.—

"A Miss Johnson, who works for the same company that I work for, was married a few weeks ago and she invited me to her wedding. On the day that I had planned to buy a wedding gift for her I brought the wedding invitation with me so that I would have the address to which the gift was to be delivered. Later that day I went to one of the downtown stores and, having made what I thought was a good selection, I pulled out the invitation to give the sales lady the address. But I noticed that Miss Johnson's home address wasn't on the invitation. There was only the address of the church where the wedding was to take place and the address of the hall where the reception was to be held. For some reason I guess I had thought that the reception was to be held at the bride's home.

"I became a little embarrassed but I thought I remembered that Miss Johnson's father's first name was 'Wayne' so that, since I knew the locality where they lived, I thought I could look up the address in the phone book. The sales lady obligingly gave me one but I found that none of the 'Wayne Johnsons' lived in the right locality. Then I suddenly remembered that 'Wayne' was the groom's name, not the father's name. Again I became embarrassed. I asked the sales lady if she would hold the gift a few minutes while I made a phone call to find out the correct address. She replied good naturedly that she would.

"By this time I could notice that I was becoming pretty tense but I commanded my muscles to walk slowly to the nearest phone, where I intended to call the company where I work to find out Miss Johnson's address. Then, just as I was about to put the dime in the phone box, it occurred to me that the father's first name must be on the wedding invitation. I looked and there it was, 'Alfred.' After that it was a very simple matter to look up the bride's address.

"When I returned to the sales lady she said, smiling, 'Well, it didn't take you long did it?' 'No,' I replied, feeling my face blush a little, with the thought of self blame for the mistakes I had made rising up in my mind. But even while she wrote out the sales ticket and I wrote out a card to go with the gift, my Recovery training began to come to the fore. I spotted my experience in the store as being average. I knew that it is average to forget addresses and to confuse names. I knew, also, that with a sense of humor I should be able to view my mistakes as trivial and myself as average.

"My Recovery training has enabled me to reject the thought of self blame for trivial mistakes and to check the working up process. I no longer make an all-out, sustained condemnation of my mental capacity—as I did in pre-Recovery days—with the result that I now avoid the mounting tenseness and the severe symptoms."

Dr. Low's Comment:

Phil says: "I knew it is average to forget addresses and to confuse names. I knew, also, that...I should be able to view my mistakes as trivial and myself as average." This reminds me that I know how silly it is to worry; I know, also, that worry does much harm and gives little aid; I know all of this but hardly an hour passes in my life but I worry—about myself, my future, my family, my patients. I could mention other things which I know I should not do, yet, I do them, one of them being smoking, another getting angry, a third blaming myself for banal offenses. I know but the knowledge helps little. You know, Phil, what I am driving at because I have mentioned it so frequently: Knowledge is good and indispensable for action and planning. But with all the knowledge of the good you will bungle and slip and frequently do the bad. The reason is that after you have learned and know the good you must practice and practice and practice again what you know. It is practice that gives you the skill, the assurance and mastery for correct action. Knowledge teaches you *what* to do, but practice tells you *how* to do it. This goes for ordinary performances, but also for such complex conduct as the art of acting average, the skill in avoiding self-diagnosis and holding down temper. All the theoretical knowledge you may have about them will avail you little unless you add practical training—in self-control. And one of the great accomplishments of our Recovery techniques has been to deflate the value of knowledge and to emphasize the supreme importance of training, and continuous training at that. The continuous training, guided by continuous spotting, yields what we will call: self-management and self-control, both of which combine to furnish self-help.

2. Chicago, Illinois—Ann L.
[Decision To Bear Discomfort]

Ann L.:

"On our way to church one Sunday my husband told me he would have to stay after the services to attend a meeting. I instantly became angry. I told him he should have let me know about the meeting earlier as I had a roast, with potatoes in the oven and had asked our daughter and her husband to come for dinner promptly at 12:30.

"My husband suggested that I drive the car home. He said that he would come home with one of the other members of the congregation. To this I replied, in temper, 'but you know how I hate to drive in heavy traffic.'

"At this point we were about to enter the church so our discussion was terminated. After we had taken our seats I noticed that I had symptoms—hand tremors, preoccupation, and I felt very self-conscious. Realizing, then, that I had been indulging in temper, I made up my mind that I would solidly reject the idea that my husband was wrong for not informing me earlier about the meeting. I decided that I would 'bear the discomfort' of driving home alone and of keeping my husband's dinner warm for him until he arrived.

"Within a few minutes after I decided to discard my temper the symptoms left and I was able to appreciate the services. Before Recovery I would have vacillated back and forth between blaming my husband and not blaming him and the symptoms would have gone on and on."

Dr. Low's Comment:

None because the example speaks for itself. It is to the point, brief and well modeled after the official pattern.

3. *Muscatine, Iowa—Ernest H.*
[Self-Control and Group Obligation]

Ernest H., Branch Leader:

"The thing happened in 1945. I had just returned from Chicago where Dr. Low had treated me at St. Joseph's Hospital. We were invited to a dinner party given by a local physician. There were upward of fifty guests present. I had known most of them for years but now I had difficulty remembering their names. This scared me. Suddenly I thought I heard a lady whispering, 'He just got home from an insane asylum.' I tensed up and when a waitress came by and said, 'Hello, Ernest,' my answer was 'Good morning,' and here it was evening. I recognized my mistake in a flash, but my discomfort turned into a panic. Then I made a clumsy movement with my arm, and my fork fell to the floor. It seemed there was no end to my bungling, and the more bungling the more tenseness, and the more tenseness the more bungling. A vicious cycle had set in.

"Going home I blamed my wife for the discomfort. She said I imagined that people talked about me. I said I didn't imagine. Finally I contradicted everything she said or tried to say. The arguments were kept up for days and grew more violent every day. In the end I was taken back to Chicago for more treatment. I had suffered a relapse. At that time I was not aware of my temper causing the return to the hospital.

"Seven years later: My daughter came home this last summer and said she was planning on being married shortly. This did not upset me. She then confided to us that she planned on a church wedding. This was all right with me till she added: 'You'll have to walk down the aisle and give me away.' With this I jumped up and said, 'There is going to be no Astor wedding in our clan.' My wife came back quickly, 'This isn't your wedding and if those are her plans, you'll have to fit in with them.' In a fraction of a second I spotted my reaction as TEMPER. I was still disturbed and answered with a disgruntled 'all right.' Then I sat down and listened.

"The night of the wedding I was tense and had palpitations, sweating, air-hunger and shaking knees. But I said to myself: Ernest, you are having lots of discomfort. But you know Dr. Low is not interested in symptoms but how you handle them through your muscles. Do you guide your impulses by personal whim or by group obligation?

"Well, as I walked down the aisle I still had my symptoms but they were decidedly guided by my sense of group obligations. When we left the church the symptoms were gone and I gave myself a plus for self-control. Recovery has made this possible for me. It took me seven years to reach this degree of control but, believe me, it was worth it."

Dr. Low's Comment:

I have nothing to add to this example of skill and polish which is a perfect demonstration of how a panel example should be constructed.

4. Brighton, Michigan—Marge H.
[Practicing the Courage to Make Mistakes]

Marge H.—

Marge hesitated to give the following example for she felt maybe even Recovery members would feel she had been exceptionally "dumb." However, after she gave the example everyone agreed that they had suffered the same feelings at one time or another.

Here is the example:

On a past election day Marge went down to vote and she said she felt a little tense even before she went into the building. When she gave her name to one of the helpers the lady said that she would have to go to someone else because she didn't have her name. Then, in a helpful mood, she called to one of the other workers. Now it seemed to Marge, at the time, that everyone was yelling back and forth when actually, she said, they were probably talking in a normal tone of voice. At any rate Marge felt she had drawn considerable attention from everyone present.

She finally got straightened out and started into the voting booth. Feeling somewhat rattled, she remembered that she didn't have a pencil with her. She asked one of the workers if she could borrow his pencil. He gave it to her and she took a few steps when someone called out for her not to use that pencil, that indelible pencils were provided in the booth. She could feel herself blushing a little and felt like a complete moron. It seemed to her she had upset the whole place with her stupidity. When she was confronted with the confusing list of names on the ballot she felt all the more helpless but she managed to cast her vote and leave.

It took Marge, who is an expert spotter, a little while to realize that she had to have the courage to make mistakes. She still didn't feel quite right about it until she was assured by other Recovery members that what she had gone through was quite "average."

Dr. Low's Comment:

None needed, except that I am always amazed to see how quickly a newcomer to our branches manages to exhibit a fine grasp of our techniques and an exquisite adroitness in practicing them. Congratulations, Marge!

5. Brighton, Michigan—Ruth H.
[Conquering Fear of Contamination]

Ruth H.—

Ruth has had ample opportunity to prove that she has conquered her morbid fear of germs. She has recently returned to a job as waitress, after an absence of five years.

When Ruth first came to Recovery her viewpoint was that anyone who even stepped into her home was "contaminated" and anything that the person touched would have to be scrubbed and disinfected before Ruth would feel comfortable again. For Ruth to venture outside of the house was next to impossible. When even door knobs, water faucets, etc. had to be handled only with the protection of kleenex, how was it possible to go to stores or to the post office or even handle the children after they had been outside to play? Consequently, not only Ruth, but also her two children were virtually prisoners in their own home. The children were constantly warned not to touch dozens of objects and life was practically suspended.

But Ruth took to Recovery with a will. She refused to miss a meeting; she read, studied and practiced. Now, after a few months of training, Ruth is back at work in a restaurant. Her fear of germs is gone.

She has learned in Recovery (1) That other patients in that group have conquered similar obsessions. (2) That her horror of being "contaminated" or "contaminating" others were nothing but frightening sensations. And she practiced the Recovery slogan of: Sensations are distressing but not dangerous. (3) That muscles can be commanded to do what one fears to do. She has learned that she can handle both fearful and angry temper. (The job of being a waitress provides many opportunities for a nervous patient to be both fearful and angry.)

Recently, when Ruth was forced to make an unexpected trip to Detroit, she rode the bus, street cars, and taxis. She confessed that she did feel some discomfort because these conveyances had been her worst source of fear, being liable to "contamination" by every passenger. But she never at any time doubted that her muscles would carry her through. Ruth is a beautiful example of what Recovery can do if one has a firm determination to get well.

Dr. Low's Comment:

Ruth's example is little short of inspiring. What she suffered from and Treasure describes so expertly was one of those obsessions which causes patients to have a horror of dirt, germs, poisons or anything that can "contaminate" them or others. Let me state that these obsessions are of the most difficult in point of treatment. If I mention that I have never been able to effect a cure or even a noticeable improvement of this condition through office treatment alone, and that in Recovery I have been able to cure dozens of these helpless sufferers, you will realize that it is precisely these frightful obsessions that prove how efficient are our group techniques. I have nothing else to add to Treasure's splendid description and to Ruth's superb performance.

6. Brighton, Michigan—Treasure R.
[Desire for Perfect Achievement]

Treasure R., Branch Leader:

"I am glad I was asked to serve on the panel when I was in Chicago one Saturday last August. I had an original response of fright, when I was asked, but when I gave my example I was quite comfortable.

"But doubt came later and I was sorry I had chosen the particular example that I gave. I immediately thought of another one that would have fit the panel subject better, it seemed to me. But I knew that if it was a mistake to have given that particular example I can afford to make mistakes because I am average. I spotted my Romantic Ambition (topic for the day).

"Then, after the panel discussion was over, I felt better when one of the girls came over and told me that my example really helped her."

Dr. Low's Comment:

In my opinion there is no better training ground for practicing Recovery principles than the panel discussion. Even with me who has delivered over 1,500 addresses before Recovery gatherings (twice weekly for fifteen years) there is still some fearful anticipation before each speech and a good deal of unfavorable self-critique afterwards. Neither I nor Treasure nor anyone else will ever lose this bent for gruesome prognosis and depressing post-mortem. It is human nature to want superior performance and the perfect achievement. Hence, if you have to give a panel example you do not relish the thought that your mental production was average. You want it to be striking, singular, exceptional. This is your and my and everybody's nature. And unless you manage to be saint, angel and wizard combined, you will never succeed in getting rid of your nature. Nature cannot be expelled, but in Recovery we have learned that nature can be controlled. When you developed your fear and self-pity after delivering your panel example, Treasure, you acted out your nature. When you spotted your "Romantic Action" you controlled that same nature. Your taking part in the panel helped you (1) to become aware of your nature, (2) to control it, (3) to help a poor creature who looked for help.

1. *Chicago, Illinois—Frank R.*
[Undesirable Exceptionality]

Frank R.—

"When I first started giving examples on the Saturday afternoon and Home Meeting Panels, I had great difficulty in selecting what I thought were suitable examples. I had the idea that for an example to be a good one it should deal with a momentous event. Unless it dealt with an exceptional, extraordinary, or emergency situation I did not consider it to be a suitable example. And my first examples were along this line. If I cancelled an appointment with Dr. Low I thought that he would refuse to accept me as a patient any longer. If I got a cold I always thought that it would lead to pneumonia. If I made a mistake at work I thought that I would be fired. If I slept poorly during the night, I thought that I would collapse physically the next day. If I was late for an appointment with a friend, I thought that I would lose his friendship forever. If I forgot to mail a letter, then I was sure I was losing my mind. If my appetite was poor, I was sure that I would develop a very serious case of malnutrition. Thus I always looked for big things on which to base my examples.

"It wasn't long before I had exhausted my supply of 'big' examples and then I was stymied. It became almost impossible for me to choose one. One day I was asked to sit on the Saturday afternoon panel on short notice. I did and I gave an example. In considering the example afterwards I noticed with surprise that I had not dealt with anything 'big.' I told how the barking of the dog next door was a constant source of irritation to me. Then came to my mind what is constantly emphasized in Recovery and that is 'average life consists of trivialities mainly.' From then on I ignored the big things of life and looked for my examples in the countless trivialities of everyday life. Here I found an inexhaustible source of examples."

Dr. Low's Comment:

Frank touches on a most important subject. He describes how, in the past, everything he did or failed to do appeared likely to lead to an emergency. He quotes as an example the desire or necessity to cancel an appointment with me. This was considered a grave danger because I might refuse to grant another appointment. Other examples were: A cold was thought to be the inevitable forerunner of a pneumonia; a mistake made on the job carried with it the threat of dismissal. Poor sleep was certain to lead to physical collapse. Diminished appetite conjured up the gruesome vision of death from malnutrition, and forgetting meant a mind doomed to crumble. In other words, Frank, in those days, considered himself so fragile that he viewed even trifling disturbances as threatening either death or serious disease. He knows now that this is what we in Recovery call "undesirable exceptionality." Having acquired this knowledge, he now laughs at his former gullibility. But I ask: Why did Frank fail to laugh at his self-diagnosing before he had his Recovery training? He had in those confused days the same good mind that he has now. Why did he fail to use it? You, the readers of "Recovery News," know the answer: Sabotage through blindspotting. If you ask why Frank blindspotted, I shall refer you to the third part of "Mental Health" where I describe the reasons why nervous patients refuse to admit that theirs is a nervous ailment. I mention there among other things that the nervous patient "hopes" that his trouble is romantically dangerous and—hope of hopes!—that it is perhaps a severe organic condition which entails no disgrace or stigmatization. This is self-deception, of course. More than that, the self-deception is planned, deliberate and systematic. I make this harsh statement on the basis of the following consideration: If I behold a table in front of me and insist it is not a table, the denial can be nothing else but the deliberate attempt to ignore the existence or presence of an obvious fact. The denial is made for the benefit of either oneself or others. If it is addressed to others it is plain deception; if it is meant to hide a fact before oneself it is self-deception. Now, if a patient states that a night of poor sleep will lead to collapse, the exaggeration of the element of danger is so monstrous and the denial of other possibilities so obvious that no patient can have any difficulty realizing, if he wants to realize it, that his assumption is absurd. All he would have to do in order to see the absurdity is to remember that he had hundreds of poor nights and collapsed not once. The harmlessness of poor sleep for health ought to be a firm conviction with him if he *wanted* and cared to be convinced. But the patient does not want to be convinced that his symptoms are harmless. His convictions tend the opposite way. What he wants to see and believe is the emergency nature of his condition, not its harmlessness. The element of emergency he spotlights, the element of harmlessness he blindspots. And if day after day and night after night he endeavors frantically and strains energetically to deny the harmlessness and to affirm the seriousness of his symptoms, then, I am justified in saying that his blindspotting is self-deception, planned, deliberate and systematic. (See article on "Blindspotting and Spotlighting" in Recovery News, August 1950).

How clearly patients understand the imbecility of their fears is evident from a little experiment which I am fond of practicing on the many saboteurs who come to my office. I tell them: Mr. Smith, a patient of mine, has complained of poor sleep for many years. Today he told me that last night he could get no sleep at all. He now fears he will collapse. Do you believe he will? Most patients, caught off guard, promptly reply: That is impossible. One night of sleeplessness couldn't do that. The absurdities voiced by others the patients spotlight; their own absurdities they blindspot. I wish that all my patients performed this little experiment on themselves. When they fear that their dizziness or numbness will lead them to destruction, I wish they would ask themselves the question: If Mr. X had my dizziness or numbness and feared they will kill him or cripple him, would I believe that? If you ask this question all the time you might be well all the time.

2. Brighton, Michigan—Jerry L.
[Expectations and Disappointments]

Jerry L.—

Jerry is a new member and everyone in the Brighton branch is congratulating him these days for the beautiful job he has done with Recovery. Jerry had the fear of physical collapse and was visiting the doctor several times a week. Each time he was sure he was dying. However, the doctor did not share this belief and Jerry was told that there was nothing wrong with him.

This assurance that everything was all right would last for a few days, until Jerry's heart would begin to pound and a new panic would develop. Then would come the flight from work to the doctor's office and ditto the doctor's diagnosis of—nothing wrong.

Then Jerry heard about Recovery. Well, the story is familiar to Recovery members but it always bears repeating. Within a few short months Jerry had his panics conquered and his temper under control. Here is an example of the way Jerry practices: He went hunting the other day and bagged two squirrels. Being group minded now, because of his Recovery training, he told his wife that he would clean the game and prepare dinner himself. Well, Jerry says that anyone who has ever cleaned a squirrel will agree that it is a most difficult job but Jerry practiced Recovery and controlled his temper through the frustration and irritation of cleaning the animals. When the meal was in the frying pan he went to the basement to take care of something. After a bit he smelled something burning, rushed up to the kitchen to find everything scorched.

Jerry admitted that he indulged in a bit of sabotage then (temper), but quickly salvaged what he could of the meal and, instead of brooding over the mistake, laughed it off.

Prior to Recovery, Jerry told the other members, he probably would have hurled the frying pan and its contents at the nearest wall (or something of this sort) and would have worked himself up for days afterward. As it was, Jerry, because of self-control at the time, had no after effect from his experience.

Dr. Low's Comment:

This is a fine illustration of the close linkage between temper and symptoms. Jerry's fearful temper was likely to be kept alive all the time by the alarming nature of his palpitations and air-hunger. His angry temper was apt to be aroused just as frequently by the "frustrations and irritations" of animals difficult to be cleaned, by dishes burning and scorching and by any kind of performance in which the object worked on obstructed the effort. In his pre-Recovery days, Jerry was forever brimming with fear and anger when symptoms kicked up or squirrels refused to be cleaned or dishes chose to get scorched. He obviously did what all patients do when untrained: He expected symptoms not to cause disturbance, squirrels to be docile and dishes to avoid spoilage carefully and diligently. Expectations of this description are clearly exceptional.

And if a person expects to live in a world purged of frustrations and obstructions, his extravagant *expectations* will of necessity invite *disappointments*. Then tempers will rise abundantly, and symptoms will not go down rapidly. In his pre-Recovery days, Jerry entertained unrealistic expectations which were currently disappointed by a cruel reality. Today, having gone through the process of Recovery training, he has turned realist and, living an average existence, expects average results and is seldom disappointed by equally average frustrations.

1. *Brighton, Michigan—Treasure R.*
[Inner Responses and Outer Reactions]

Treasure R.—

"When I first started to lead our Brighton, Mich. group, it didn't take me long to find out that there was a vast difference between watching a well conducted panel meeting in Chicago and doing it myself. When our group had grown to a size of 7 or 8 members we would always begin by reading one of the articles from the Recovery literature. Then I would usually give an example of my own. . . . Reaction of the group—dead silence! Followed by a few embarrassed giggles. After that it was anybody's guess what we would talk about for the remainder of the evening. I guess, maybe, the discussion of Recovery principles did come in for at least a small share of the time—back in our early days—but such things as baseball, the latest in women's fashions, politics, etc., were the main topics of conversation.

"This hit-or-miss method of conducting panels made me feel very uneasy because I realized that our time at the meetings should be properly utilized if we were to get the help that we all needed. After a few more trips to Chicago, however, I began to acquire more confidence in my ability as a leader. So, when I would be confronted with dead silence from the others, after requesting some examples, I would single out one member and say: 'How have you been lately?' (Sometimes this question got me nowhere either, when the member answered: 'Just fine, thank you.') But nine times out of ten I found that, if you ask a nervous patient how he is, he will not hesitate to tell you about whatever difficulties he may be experiencing at the time.

"Of course, just the first few words that the patient utters are enough to start the ball rolling. Usually, before he stops speaking, you have *several* examples. This in turn pops the thought of a similar happening into the head of another patient, etc., etc.

"I have discovered that the individual examples are absolutely necessary in order to demonstrate the Recovery method properly. I, for one, am not gifted as a public speaker, even on such a dear-to-my-heart subject as Recovery, and so without the participation of at least a few of the members I am not anywhere near as effective a group leader as I should be.

"After five years of experience in conducting Recovery meetings there are still occasions when I feel that the meeting was not up to par. But usually I am more than satisfied with the outcome. At each get-together that we have my main objective is to see that at least one point has been 'driven home.' I have developed some skill, too, at seeing to it that we stick to the subject of Recovery—at least until refreshments are served. The other night it happened that we somehow drifted into the time-consuming subject of house breaking small puppies. It was not until one of the members said, in the course of his conversation, that he had kicked his pup, that I could break in and say—'Ah, did you have temper?' Then we were back on the right track.

"Of course, after a few of our members became *veteran* members, the examples were much more easily obtained. Now I can always rely on a few of our 'old hands' to come through with a good example. If, as it sometimes happens, I find it difficult to give an example of my own, I always know that I am trying for exceptionality. I have found that simple examples that deal with such down to earth things as mislayed tooth paste caps, unfilled sugar bowls, etc., are the best. And need I mention that good Recovery examples dealing with trivial items such as these happen to all of us every day?''

Dr. Low's Comment:

This little treatise on how to get panel examples is neat and tidy and thought-provoking. The thoughts which it provoked in me were as follows: When Treasure humbly declares that she is "not gifted as a public speaker," I have nothing to offer, either in assent or dissent. But in Recovery there is no need for *public speaking*, there is a call for *private spotting*. And my final verdict, derived from many years of association with and observation of our Michigan leader is that her speaking, public or otherwise, is clear, to the point and effective, and her spotting, privately conducted in her inner environment, is a superb achievement in Self-Help, a successful record of group leadership and self-steering.

Another thought which Treasure provoked in me was occasioned by her remark that she is "not nearly as effective a group leader" as she ought to be. This utterly unfair self-appraisal provoked my thoughts but also surprise and some resentment. Good

Heavens, I surmised, how effective does Treasure want to be! Does she aspire to a record of peak performance? If she does, then, her ideal is exceptionality, and not averageness. In the case of Treasure, this is a grave slip because, as I see it, her averageness is of such high quality that she could safely afford to rest content with her achievement.

Don't mind, Treasure, if I proceed to rib you some more. "After five years of experience in conducting Recovery meetings," you say, "there are still occasions when I feel that the meeting was not up to par." This is quite tragic, I admit. But the tragedy is not peculiar to you, Treasure, but to the human race. It is a tragic experience of my own. For instance, I have conducted at least two group meetings every week since 1933, that is, twenty years. That adds up to a total of about 2,000 meetings. Don't you think my performance ought to be tops by now? It ought to, but it isn't. At any rate, it isn't such in my own eyes. I still indulge in vicious self-criticism, still think I don't do well enough, and the thought still torments me "on some occasions" that "the meeting was not up to par." You see, Treasure, both you and I are human, and humans have never been known to endorse themselves as they should. Their first impulse is to release self-critical responses. You know that responses of any kind stem from a person's temperament, and it is the inner responses of temperament which continually generate impulses of exceptionality, self-distrust and self-belittling. It is a tragedy but can be turned into a comedy if humor steps in and converts a *self-critical inner response* into a *self-endorsing outer reaction*. Somewhere I have said: All men are alike in their inner responses; they differ in their outer reactions. Moreover, the inner responses are your nature. Are you going to change your nature? The Latins used to say: You cannot expel nature, not even if you use a pitchfork. Well, the Latins were right, and nature cannot be changed, and natural responses will always be what they are. But in Recovery both you and I have learned that though natural responses are immune to changing, yet, they are amenable to spotting. And let me assure you, Treasure, that in the field of spotting, you have achieved a degree of expertness that stands you in good stead. You demonstrated your spotting efficiency when you stated: "I always know that I am trying for exceptionality." If you know that and know it "always," you certainly qualify for Recovery leadership.